If God Were a Human Rights Activist

Stanford Studies in Human Rights

If God Were
a Human Rights Activist

Boaventura de Sousa Santos

Stanford University Press
Stanford, California

Stanford University Press
Stanford, California

Printed in the United States of America on acid-free, archival-quality paper

Library of Congress Cataloging-in-Publication Data

Santos, Boaventura de Sousa, author.
If God were a human rights activist / Boaventura de Sousa Santos.
  pages cm
Includes bibliographical references and index.
ISBN 978-0-8047-9326-1 (cloth : alk. paper)—
ISBN 978-0-8047-9500-5 (pbk. : alk. paper)
1. Human rights—Religious aspects. 2. Political theology. I. Title.
BL65.H78S26 2015
323.01—dc23
2014038924

ISBN 978-0-8047-9503-6 (electronic)

Typeset by Bruce Lundquist in 10/14 Minion Pro

For M.I.R.

Contents

Foreword

BOAVENTURA DE SOUSA SANTOS'S *If God Were a Human Rights Activist* is a tour de force of the moral and intellectual imagination. In both the creativity of its several key lines of argument, and in the way historical, political, and cultural lines of evidence are parsed, interrogated, and, finally, synthesized in bold and even startling ways, the book breaks new ground and points the way toward the possibility of alternative practices anchored in what Santos calls "relational" grammars of human dignity.

In this wide-ranging critique and emergent reconstruction of human rights, Santos develops a mode of engagement that goes beyond mere inter-disciplinarity. Although his study is deeply rooted in the tradition of academic writing, the questions he takes up, and the framework he reveals for answering them, suggest an ecology that ranges beyond the walls of the academy, across the lines that divide the Global North from the Global South, and against cen-turies of oppression based on forms of what Santos describes as "cognitive injustice." Paradoxically, one of these forms of cognitive injustice has been what he calls the "conventional" understanding and practice of human rights, particularly after the end of the Cold War. Although, as he argues, human rights orthodoxy has not taken hold everywhere with the same force or in the same way (one thinks of China and the United States as key outliers), never-theless, the conventional account is shaping the contemporary world on its way to hegemony. ("Conventional," as Santos uses it here, is meant to mark the moment in history in which human rights are, as he puts it, "less than hege-monic and more than dominant" in the often coercive role it plays in societies around the world.)

In Santos's analysis, conventional human rights shape consequential forms of action in the contemporary world on the basis of four illusions. For Santos, the critical task is to deconstruct these illusions so that the productive and even potentially emancipatory core of human rights can be repurposed as an epistemological and ethical resource within struggles of liberation and cognitive self-determination. First, according to Santos, the discourse of human rights suggests its own inevitability despite its actual historical contingency, even after the Universal Declaration of Human Rights was promulgated in 1948 as a fait accompli. If it is true, as the human rights scholar and anthropologist Richard A. Wilson has argued, that human rights have become the "archetypal language of democratic transition" (2001: 1), then for Santos it is important to acknowledge that this was the result of a string of idiosyncratic and nonessential events in history, politics, and the global economy; in other words, it could have been (and it might be in the future) otherwise. Second, the rise of human rights, again, particularly after the end of the Cold War (and, even more, after the end of the post–Cold War) has been accompanied by a wide-ranging elision of alternative visions of justice, particularly those associated with religious and nationalist ideologies. Nevertheless, if human rights have become dominant, Santos argues, this position should not be taken as a reflection of its inherent superiority. Third, like other universalisms in history, human rights are infused with an abstractness that obscures all of the important contexts that make it meaningful, concrete, and contradictory in actual social practice. And finally, and perhaps most importantly, Santos draws our attention to the illusion that conventional human rights are monolithic when in fact even dominant understandings and practices of human rights contain a diversity of conceptual emphasis, historical emergence, and cultural resonance.

For Santos, the empirical fact of human rights pluralism holds the key to the synthesis he develops in *If God Were a Human Rights Activist.* It allows him to use a practical and grounded hermeneutics to reveal the ways in which a more heterodox, that is, actual, account of human rights shares overlapping claims about human dignity with important strains of religious doctrine. As he argues, the hermeneutic engagement with dominant contemporary world religions— which represent, for Santos, the clearest alternatives to human rights—shows them to be a surprising potential "source of radical energy toward counter-hegemonic human rights struggles."

At a moment in history in which, as he puts it, "the most appalling social injustices and unjust human suffering no longer seem to generate . . . moral indignation," what is urgently needed is the willingness to subject our most hallowed grammars of human dignity to careful and creative scrutiny, for, as Santos convincingly shows us, these have more often than not often failed to translate into enduring practices of resistance for the world's most vulnerable and marginalized populations. *If God Were a Human Rights Activist* is precisely such an urgent and necessary reappraisal.

Series Editor Mark Goodale

Preface

WE LIVE IN A TIME dominated by the power of the idea of individual autonomy, an autonomy that is to be exercised in a planetary marketplace constituted by a myriad of local, national, and global markets in which potentially
all dimensions of individual and social life are traded according to their price-
tagged value. According to this idea, society consists of supposedly self-made
individuals whose life chances depend almost entirely on themselves, for better or for worse. These life chances are determined by life choices to be exercised through infinite options of exit (to use Albert Hirschman's well-known
concept) *within* the planetary marketplace. The only unavailable option is the
exit *from* the planetary marketplace. This idea is an ideology to the extent
that it underwrites, manifests, and reinforces the dominant power relations
in our societies. It operates as a kind of normative apolitics: *normative* because people are asked, if not forced, to be autonomous—only to be utterly
abandoned if their failures are seen as the result of ineptitude in the exercise
of their autonomy; *apolitical* because the immense power of this idea consists
in promoting an idea of power as immensely fragmented, as disseminated
in a virtually infinite web of interactions among individuals competing for
scarce resources and rewards in the marketplace. Individual autonomy is thus
understood as personal engagement with a ready-made, unchangeable world.
The asocial or even antisocial being thus constituted is the *homo sociologicus*
of global monopoly capitalism—or neoliberalism, as it is usually called—a
much-expanded version of the *homo economicus*. Disseminated by prosely-
tizers who believe that their mission is to announce the new way of being
human, this ideology prevails all over the world, even though the impact of its
penetration varies widely from region to region. It is the ideological form of a
poststate, postsocial, extremely concentrated structural power through which

the 1 percent global elite rules the 99 percent impoverished world population. As an ideology, its strength resides in its performative value, not in its truth content. Actually, the promise/imposition of autonomy is doubly treacherous. First, because no one in society depends solely on him- or herself for anything other than elementary tasks (and even this is a matter of dispute). Second, because there is no autonomy without conditions of autonomy, and the latter are distributed unequally in society; moreover, in an era of neoliberal economics and politics, the individuals that are most pressed to be autonomous are precisely those most deprived of the conditions that would enable them to be so. The outcomes resulting from policies founded on this ideology are disturbing. We live in a time when the most appalling social injustices and most unjust human suffering no longer seem to generate the moral indignation and the political will necessary both to combat them effectively and to create a more just and fair society. Under such circumstances, it seems evident that we cannot afford to waste any genuine social experience of indignation that is capable of strengthening the organization and the determination of all those who have not given up the struggle for a more just society.

Counteracting the ideology of possessive individualistic autonomy, two main normative politics seem to be in place: *human rights* and *political theologies*. Although they are unequally present in the different regions of the globe, they both operate globally. No matter how far back one traces its ancestry, the fact is that human rights entered national and international agendas as a decisive grammar of human dignity only in the 1970s and 1980s. At the same time we were also witnessing the emergence of another normative politics, political theologies, understood as theologies that challenge the separation between the public and private spheres and that demand a role for religion in the public sphere. According to them, human dignity consists in carrying out the will of God, a mandate that cannot be restricted to the private sphere.

These two normative politics could not be farther apart. Human rights are individualistic, secular, culturally Western-centric, and state-centric, in the sense of either controlling the state or taking advantage of it. Political theologies, on the other hand, are communitarian and antisecular, may be either Western or fiercely anti-Western, and are largely hostile to the state.[1] As I show in this book, these general characterizations do not account for the internal diversity of either human rights or political theologies. On the basis of the complexity that emerges from such diversity, I pursue a kind of intercultural translation between these two normative politics, seeking translational zones of contact that will yield new or renewed energies for radical, progressive social transformation.

I proceed by identifying the major challenges that the rise of political theologies at the beginning of the twenty-first century poses to human rights. I then select, within a broad landscape of theological analysis, the types of reflections and practices that might contribute to expand and deepen the canon of human rights politics. With this purpose in mind, I make distinctions from which significant consequences are drawn: on the one side, distinctions among different types of political theologies (such as pluralist versus fundamentalist, traditionalist versus progressive); on the other, distinctions between two contrasting discourses and practices of human rights politics (such as hegemonic versus counterhegemonic). I end the book by arguing that pluralist and progressive theologies may be a source of radical energy toward counterhegemonic human rights struggles.

This analytical and political trajectory is not the product of a disinterested inquiry aiming only to generate still one more vanguard theory. While actively participating in the World Social Forum (Santos, 2006b) I have often observed how activists fighting for socioeconomic, historical, sexual, racial, cultural, and postcolonial justice would frequently base their activism and their claims on Christian, Islamic, Judaic, Hindu, Buddhist, and indigenous religious beliefs and spiritualities. In a sense, such stances bear witness to a political intersubjectivity that seems to have deserted conventional, secular critical thinking and political action; that is, the combination of creative effervescence and intense and passionate energy, on the one side, with a pluralistic, open-ended, and nonviolent conception of struggle, on the other. My aim in writing this book is to account for and strengthen such struggles, and last but not least to give sense to my participation in them.

Acknowledgments

AN EARLIER and much shorter version of this book was published in the on-line journal *Law, Social Justice and Global Development*.[2] I want to thank its editors and, in particular, Abdul Paliwala for all the support I received from him in preparing the manuscript. Since then, I have considerably expanded my argument into the book I here present. In this task I counted on the support of a group of excellent and dedicated colleagues. As always, Maria Irene Ramalho read and commented on the different versions of this work. Without the encouragement, enthusiasm, and research support of Teresa Toldy this book would never be published. Herself a noted feminist theologian, she was generous enough to dedicate much of her precious time to a book in the power of whose message she at times believed more than I myself. André Barroso, a postdoctoral student at Centro de Estudos Sociais (CES; Center for Social Studies) of the University of Coimbra, Portugal, also contributed with highly professional bibliographical suggestions. Maria Paula Meneses gave me precious research support in framing the analysis of the rise of Christian theologies in the African context. Margarida Gomes, my research assistant of many years, prepared the final version for publication with her usual care and professionalism. To all of them my most sincere thanks.

This book was developed within the framework of the research project "ALICE—Strange Mirrors, Unsuspected Lessons" (alice.ces.uc.pt) that I coordinate at CES. The project has received funding from the European Research Council under the European Union's Seventh Framework Programme (FP/2007-2013)/ERC Grant Agreement n. 269807.

If God Were a Human Rights Activist

Chapter 1

Human Rights

A Fragile Hegemony

THERE IS NO QUESTION TODAY about the global hegemony of human rights as a discourse of human dignity.[1] Nonetheless, such hegemony faces a disturbing reality. A large majority of the world's inhabitants are not the subjects of human rights. They are rather the objects of human rights discourses. The question is, then, whether human rights are efficacious in helping the struggles of the excluded, the exploited, and the discriminated against, or whether, on the contrary, they make those struggles more difficult. In other words, is the hegemony claimed by human rights today the outcome of a historical victory, or rather of a historical defeat? Regardless of the answer, human rights are the hegemonic discourse of human dignity and thus insurmountable. This explains why oppressed social groups cannot help but ask the following questions: Even if human rights are part of the selfsame hegemony that consolidates and legitimates their oppression, could they be used to subvert it? Could human rights be used in a counterhegemonic way? If so, how? These questions lead to two others: Why is so much unjust human suffering not considered a violation of human rights? What other discourses of human dignity are there in the world, and to what extent are they compatible with human rights discourses?

The search for a counterhegemonic conception of human rights must start from a hermeneutics of suspicion regarding human rights as they are conventionally understood and sustained, that is to say, concerning the conceptions of human rights that are more closely related to their Western, liberal matrix.[2] The hermeneutics of suspicion I propose is very much indebted to Ernst Bloch ([1947] 1995), who, for example, wonders about the reasons why, from the eighteenth century onward, the concept of utopia as an emancipatory political measure was gradually superseded and replaced by the concept of rights. Why was the concept of utopia less successful than the concept of law and rights as a discourse of social emancipation?[3]

We must begin by acknowledging that law and rights have a double genealogy in Western modernity. On the one hand, an abyssal genealogy. I understand the dominant versions of Western modernity as having been constructed on the basis of an abyssal thinking that divided the world sharply between metropolitan and colonial societies (Santos, 2007a). This division was such that the realities and practices existing on the other side of the line, that is, in the colonies, could not possibly challenge the universality of the theories and practices in force on the metropolitan side of the line. As such, they were made invisible. As a discourse of emancipation, human rights were historically meant to prevail only on one side of the abyssal line, that is, in the metropolitan societies. It has been my contention that this abyssal line, which produces radical exclusions, far from being eliminated with the end of historical colonialism, continues to exist and that its exclusions are carried out by other means (neocolonialism, racism, xenophobia, and the permanent state of exception in dealing with alleged terrorists, undocumented migrant workers, and asylum seekers). International law and mainstream human rights doctrines have been used to guarantee such continuity. But, on the other hand, law and rights have a revolutionary genealogy on the metropolitan side of the line. Both the American Revolution and the French Revolution were fought in the name of law and rights. Bloch maintains that the superiority of the concept of law and rights has much to do with bourgeois individualism. The bourgeois society then emerging had already conquered economic hegemony and was fighting for political hegemony, soon to be consolidated by the American and French Revolutions. The concept of law and rights fitted perfectly the emergent bourgeois individualism inherent both to liberal theory and to capitalism. It is, therefore, easy to conclude that the hegemony enjoyed by human rights has very deep roots and that its trajectory has been a linear path toward the consecration of human rights as the ruling principle of a just society. This idea of a long-established consensus manifests itself in various ways, each one of them residing in an illusion. Because they are widely shared, such illusions constitute the common sense of conventional human rights. I distinguish four illusions: teleology, triumphalism, decontextualization, and monolithism.[4]

The teleological illusion consists in reading history backwards, beginning with the consensus that exists today concerning the unconditional good human rights entail, and reading past history as a linear path inexorably leading toward such a result. The choice of precursors is crucial in this respect. As Samuel Moyn comments: "these are usable pasts: the construction of precursors after the fact" (2010: 12). Such an illusion prevents us from seeing that at any given historical moment different ideas concerning the nature of human dignity and social emancipation were in competition and that the victory of human rights is a contingent result that can be explained a posteriori, but which could not have been deterministically foreseen. The historical victory of human rights made it possible that the same actions—which according to other conceptions of human dignity would be considered actions of oppression and domination—were reconfigured as actions of emancipation and liberation when carried out in the name of human rights.

Related to the teleological illusion is the illusion of triumphalism, the notion that the victory of human rights is an unconditional human good. It takes for granted that all the other grammars of human dignity that have competed with that of human rights were inherently inferior in ethical and political terms. This Darwinian notion does not take into account a decisive feature of hegemonic Western modernity, indeed its true historical genius, namely, the way it has managed to supplement the force of the ideas that serve its purposes with the military force that, supposedly at the service of the ideas, is actually served by them. We need, therefore, to evaluate critically the grounds for the alleged ethical and political superiority of human rights. The ideals of national liberation—socialism, communism, revolution, nationalism—constituted alternative grammars of human dignity; at certain moments, they were even the dominant ones. Suffice it to say that the twentieth century's national liberation movements against colonialism, like the socialist and communist movements, did not invoke the human rights grammar to justify their causes and struggles.[5] That the other grammars and discourses of emancipation have been defeated by human rights discourses should be considered inherently positive only if it could be demonstrated that human rights, while a discourse of human emancipation, have superior merit for reasons other than the fact that they have emerged as the winner. Until then, the triumph of human rights may be considered by some as progress, a historical victory, while by others as retrogression, a historical defeat.

This precaution helps us to face the third illusion: decontextualization. It is generally acknowledged that human rights as an emancipatory discourse have their origin in eighteenth-century Enlightenment, the French Revolution, and the American Revolution. What is seldom mentioned, however, is that since then and until today human rights have been used in very distinct contexts and with contradictory objectives. In the eighteenth century, for instance, human rights were the central language of the ongoing revolutionary processes. But they were also used to legitimate practices that we would consider oppressive if not altogether counterrevolutionary. When Napoleon arrived in Egypt in 1798, this is how he explained his actions to the Egyptians: "People of Egypt: You will be told by our enemies, that I am come to destroy your religion. Believe them not. Tell them that I am come to restore your rights, punish your usurpers, and raise the true worship of Mahomet."[6] Thus was the invasion of Egypt legitimated by the invaders. The same could be said of Robespierre, who fostered the Terror during the French Revolution in the name of piety and human rights.[7] After the 1848 revolutions, human rights were no longer part of the revolution imaginary and became rather hostile to any idea of a revolutionary change of society. But the same hypocrisy (I would call it constitutive) of invoking human rights to legitimate practices that may be considered violations of human rights continued throughout the past century and a half and is perhaps more evident today than ever. From the mid-nineteenth century onward, human rights talk was separated from the revolutionary tradition and began to be conceived of as a grammar of depoliticized social change, a kind of antipolitics. At best, human rights were subsumed under the law of the state as the state established a monopoly over the production of law and the administration of justice. This is why the Russian Revolution was carried out, unlike the French and American revolutions, not in the name of law, but against law (Santos, 1995: 104–7). Gradually, the predominant discourse of human rights became the discourse of human dignity consonant with liberal politics, capitalist development, and its different metamorphoses (liberal, social-democratic, neoliberal, dependent, Fordist, post-Fordist, peripheral Fordist, corporative, state capitalism), and colonialism (neocolonialism, internal colonialism, racism, slave-like labor, xenophobia). And so we must bear in mind that the selfsame human rights discourse has had very many different meanings in different historical contexts, having legitimated both revolutionary and counterrevolutionary practices. Today we cannot even be sure if present-day human rights are a legacy of the modern revolutions or of their ruins, or if they have behind them a revolutionary, emancipatory energy or a counterrevolutionary energy.

The fourth illusion is monolithism, which is a main focus of this book. This illusion consists in denying or minimizing the tensions and even internal contradictions of the theories of human rights. Suffice it to remember that the French Revolution's Declaration of the Rights of Man is ambivalent as it speaks of the rights of *man* and of the *citizen*. From the very beginning, human rights foster ambiguity by creating belongingness to two different collective identities. One of them is humanity, supposedly an inclusive collectivity, hence *human* rights. The other is a much more restrictive collectivity, that of the citizens of a given state. This tension has burdened human rights ever since. The goal of regimes and international institutions of human rights and of the adoption of international declarations was to guarantee minimal dignity to individuals whenever their rights as members of a political collectivity did not exist or were violated. In the course of the past two hundred years, human rights were gradually incorporated into constitutions and were reconceptualized as rights of citizenship, directly guaranteed by the state and adjudicated by the courts as civic, political, social, economic, and cultural rights. But the truth is that the effective, ample protection of citizenship rights has always been precarious in the large majority of countries and, further, that human rights have been invoked mainly in situations involving the erosion or particularly serious violation of citizenship rights.[8] Human rights emerge as the lowest threshold of inclusion, a descending movement from the dense community of citizens to the diluted community of humanity. With neoliberalism and its attack on the state as the guarantor of rights, particularly social and economic rights, the community of citizens is diluted to such a degree that it becomes indistinguishable from the community of humans and citizenship rights, as trivialized as human rights. The priority granted by Hannah Arendt (1951) to citizenship rights over human rights, once pregnant with consequences, slides into normative emptiness.[9] In the process, immigrants, especially undocumented migrant workers, descend even further to the "community" of subhumans.

The other tension illustrating the illusory nature of monolithism is the one between individual and collective rights. The United Nations Universal Declaration of Human Rights, the last century's first major universal declaration, and which was followed by several others, recognizes only two lawful subjects: the individual and the state. Peoples are recognized only to the extent that they become states. When the declaration was adopted, it should be noted, there were many peoples, nations, and communities that had no state. Thus, from the point of view of the epistemologies of the South, the declaration cannot but be deemed colonialist (Burke, 2010; Terretta, 2012).[10] When we speak of equality before the law, we must bear in mind that, when the Declaration was written, individuals from vast regions of the world were not equal before the law because they were subjected to collective domination and that under collective domination individual rights provide no protection. At a time of bourgeois individualism, the Declaration could not take this into account. This was a time when sexism was part of common sense, sexual orientation was taboo, class domination was each country's internal affair, and colonialism was still strong as a historical agent, in spite of the setback constituted by India's independence. As time went by, sexism, colonialism, and the crassest forms of class domination came to be acknowledged as human rights violations. In the 1960s, anticolonial struggles were adopted by the Declaration and became part of UN affairs. However, as it was understood at the time, self-determination concerned peoples subjected to European colonialism alone. Self-determination thus understood left many peoples subjected to internal colonization, indigenous peoples being the paramount example. More than thirty years had to go by before the right of indigenous peoples to self-determination was recognized in the United Nations Declaration on the Rights of Indigenous Peoples, adopted by the General Assembly in 2007.[11] Lengthy negotiations were needed before the International Labor Organization approved Convention 169 regarding indigenous and tribal peoples. Gradually, these documents became part of the legislation of different countries.

Since collective rights are not part of the original canon of human rights, the tension between individual and collective rights results from the historical struggle of the social groups that, being excluded or discriminated against as groups, could not be adequately protected under individual human rights. The struggles of women, indigenous peoples, African people under colonial regimes, Afro-descendants, victims of racism, gays, lesbians, and religious minorities marked the past fifty years of the recognition of collective rights, a recognition that has been always highly contested and always on the verge of being reversed. There is no necessary contradiction between individual and collective rights, if for no other reason than because there are many kinds of collective rights. For instance, we can distinguish two kinds of collective rights, primary and derivative. We speak of derivative collective rights when the workers organize themselves in unions and confer upon those unions the right to represent them in negotiations with their employers. We speak of primary collective rights when a community of individuals has rights other than the rights of their organization, or renounce their individual rights on behalf of the rights of the community. These rights, in turn, may be exerted in two ways. The large majority of them are exerted individually, as when a Sikh policeman wears the turban; an Islamic female doctor wears the hijab; or a Brazilian Afro-descendent, an indigenous person, or a member of a low caste in India takes advantage of the affirmative action provided in their communities. But there are rights that can only be exerted collectively, such as the right to self-determination. Collective rights are there to eliminate or abate the insecurity and injustice suffered by individuals that are discriminated against as the systematic victims of oppression, just for being who and what they are, and not for doing what they do. Only very slowly have collective rights become part of the political agenda, whether national or international. At any rate, the contradiction or tension vis-à-vis more individualistic conceptions of human rights is always there.[12]

Bearing in mind these illusions is crucial for building a counterhegemonic conception and practice of human rights, particularly when they must be based on a dialogue with other conceptions of human dignity and the practices sustaining them. I consider the conventional understanding of human rights as having some of the following characteristics:[13] human rights are universally valid irrespective of the social, political, and cultural contexts in which they operate and of the various human rights regimes existing in different regions of the world; in our time, human rights are the only oppositional grammar and language available to confront the "pathologies of power"; the violators of human rights, no matter how horrendous the violations perpetrated, are to be punished in compliance with human rights; questioning human rights in terms of their supposed cultural or political limitations helps perpetuate the evils that human rights are designed to fight against; the recurrent phenomenon of double standards in evaluating compliance with human rights in no way compromises the universal validity of human rights; human rights are premised upon the idea of human dignity, itself grounded on a conception of human nature as individual, self-sustaining, and qualitatively different from non–human nature; freedom of religion can be secured only to the extent that the public sphere is freed from religion, which is the premise of secularism; what counts as a violation of human rights is defined by universal declarations and multilateral institutions (courts and commissions), and established global (mostly North-based) nongovernmental organizations; violations of human rights can be adequately measured according to quantitative indicators; the respect for human rights is much more problematic in the Global South than in the Global North.

The limits of this conception of human rights become obvious in the responses it gives to one of the most important questions of our time, and the perplexity it provokes grounds the impulse to construct a counterhegemonic conception of human rights as proposed in this book. The question can be formulated in this way: If humanity is one alone, why are there so many different principles concerning human dignity and a just society, all of them presumably unique, yet often contradictory among themselves? At the root of this perplexity is a recognition that much has been elided by the modern, Western understanding of the world and thus by the Western-centric conception of universal human rights.

The conventional answer to this question is that such diversity is to be recognized only to the extent that it does not contradict universal human rights. By postulating the abstract universality of the conception of human dignity that underlies human rights, this answer dismisses the perplexity underlying the question. The fact that such a conception is Western-based is considered irrelevant because, so it is claimed, the historicity of the discourse of human rights does not interfere with its ontological status.[14] Generally embraced by hegemonic political thinking, particularly in the Global North, this answer reduces the understanding of the world to the Western-centric version, thus ignoring or trivializing decisive cultural and political experiences and initiatives in the countries of the Global South. This is the case with the movements of resistance that have been emerging against oppression, marginalization, and exclusion, the ideological bases of which often have very little to do with the dominant Western cultural and political references prevalent throughout the twentieth century. These movements do not formulate their struggles in terms of human rights; rather, they formulate them at times according to principles that contradict the dominant principles of human rights. These movements are often grounded in multi-secular cultural and historical identities, often including religious militancy. It will suffice to mention three such movements, with very distinct political meanings: indigenous movements, particularly in Latin America; the peasant movements in Africa and Asia; and the Islamic insurgency. In spite of the huge differences among them, these movements all start out from cultural and political references that are non-Western, even if constituted by the resistance to Western domination.

Conventional or hegemonic human rights thinking lacks the theoretical and analytical tools necessary to position itself in relation to such movements; even worse, it does not understand the importance of doing so. It applies the same abstract recipe across the board, hoping that thereby the nature of alternative ideologies or symbolic universes will be reduced to local specificities with no impact on the universal canon of human rights.

In this book I focus on the challenges to human rights that arise when the latter are faced with movements that claim the presence of religion in the public sphere. Such movements, increasingly globalized, together with the political theologies sustaining them, constitute a grammar in defense of human dignity that rivals the one underlying human rights, and often contradicts it. As I have suggested above, the conventional or hegemonic conceptions and practices of human rights are not capable of facing these challenges, and do not even imagine it is necessary to do so. A counterhegemonic conception of human rights alone can adequately face such challenges, as I try to demonstrate throughout this book.

Chapter 2

The Globalization of Political Theologies

CLAIMING RELIGION as a constitutive element of public life has been increasingly gaining worldwide relevance in the past few decades. It is a multifaceted trend, regarding both the denominations involved and political and cultural orientations. Yet religion is pervasive throughout the world and the networks feeding it are transnational, which allows us to pronounce it a global phenomenon. Elsewhere (Santos, 1995; 2002a; 2006b; 2007c, 2008) I have argued that globalization is not a monolithic phenomenon and that transnational relations are webs of opposite globalizations that sometimes run parallel and sometimes intersect.[1] On the one hand, there is hegemonic, neoliberal globalization—the new phase of global capitalism—and the political, legal, and cultural norms that go with it (the rule of law, liberal democracy, and human rights). On the other hand, there is counterhegemonic globalization, or globalization from below. This involves the social movements and organizations that, through local, national, and global articulations, fight against capitalist, colonialist, and patriarchal oppression; social inequality and discrimination; the destruction of ecological systems and associated livelihoods; and the imposition of Western cultural norms and the destruction of non-Western ones caused or intensified by hegemonic globalization.

The hegemonic, the counterhegemonic, and the nonhegemonic

Hegemonic globalization has at its service a number of supposedly all-powerful institutions, from the G-7 to the World Bank, from the International Monetary Fund to the World Trade Organization.[2] Counterhegemonic globalization consists of transnational articulations of social movements and NGOs, be they the

World Social Forum, the Global Assembly of Social Movements, the Peoples' Summit, the Via Campesina, the World March of Women, the World Indigenous Movement, the Environmental Justice Movement, together with transnational advocacy networks on different issues.[3]

As conceived here, hegemony is a cluster of intellectual and political schemes that are viewed by most people (even by people negatively affected by them) as providing the natural or only possible understanding of social life. In turn, counterhegemony is the work of organized, countercurrent mobilizations that aim at discrediting hegemonic schemes and providing credible alternative understandings of social life.[4] What is hegemonic about globalization is not necessarily global and the same is true of what is counterhegemonic. What is hegemonic and what is counterhegemonic can only be determined contextually. A strike by trade unions or a protest by the "degrowth" movements in the Global North may be viewed in this region as countering the objectives of neoliberal globalization and, therefore, as counterhegemonic. However, the same initiatives, when viewed from the Global South, may be considered as variations within neoliberal globalization and therefore as hegemonic. These asymmetries are partially responsible for the difficulties in building North-South alliances among groups and movements that struggle for the same general goals of social emancipation and liberation. Globalization, be it hegemonic or counterhegemonic, involves not so much transcending contexts but rather transforming, reorganizing, and reconfiguring them. On the other hand, contextual difference varies in intensity across different social fields. For instance, capitalist social relations are far more univocal or context-indifferent on the economic than on the political and cultural levels. As the case of contemporary China shows, global capitalism can coexist with different political and cultural regimes, and may actually gather more power from such diversity.

As I understand it in this book, the hegemonic is in our time a global, multifaceted web of unequal economic, social, sexual, political, cultural, and epistemological relations, grounded on the interactions between three main structures of power and domination: capitalism, colonialism, and patriarchy. These structures operate through and are legitimated by a liberal understanding of the rule of law, democracy, and human rights, viewed as embodying the ideals of a good society. Conversely, the counterhegemonic consists of the struggles, movements, and initiatives that through globally recognizable discourses and practices aim at eliminating or reducing unequal power relations, transforming them into relations of shared authority. Such struggles challenge the liberal understanding of their own achievements as mystifying ideology, and propose oppositional ideals of a good society born from the struggles themselves. In some domains of global interactions the binary hegemonic/ counterhegemonic does not cover the whole field of possibilities. There are courses of action or forms of social regulation that are neither hegemonic nor counterhegemonic in the sense I am adopting here. For example, I consider nonhegemonic struggles and initiatives to be practices that resist hegemonic forms of domination and their liberal understandings, but that do so with the aim of replacing them with other forms of domination that will reproduce or even aggravate unequal social power relations. In light of this distinction, a form of social regulation that proposes the substitution of a religious state for a secular state is certainly not part of hegemonic structures of domination and their liberal understandings in most regions of the world, but neither is it counterhegemonic in the sense given here, since rather than aiming at reducing unequal power relations it is geared to replace a given pattern of unequal power relations with another one, eventually more authoritarian and unjust. Likewise, political theologies that reject the distinction between the public and private spheres and grant one given religion (and one specific interpretation of it) the privilege of organizing social and political life with exclusivity can be seen as nonhegemonic, but not as counterhegemonic in the sense given here since they—rather than confronting capitalism, colonialism, or patriarchy— oftentimes credit them with divine justification.

The Western resolution of the religious question

As I mentioned above, claiming religion as a constitutive element of public life is a growing trend in recent decades. As is the case with globalization processes in general, this is not a totally new phenomenon. Just think of the role played by Catholicism in the European colonial expansion, or that of Islam in the conquest of Persia (633–656) and in the formation and consolidation of the Ottoman Empire (1299–1922). It is new only to the extent that it is occurring after centuries of colonial and neocolonial domination, as well as in the aftermath of the global imposition of the cultural and political paradigm of Western modernity. After centuries of religious conflicts in Europe, this paradigm settled for an unprecedented resolution of the religious question, the question of the role of religion in society: On the one hand, Christian values are recognized as "universal"; on the other, institutional Christianity is relegated to the management of the private sphere, the sphere of individuals' autonomous and voluntary decisions. This

Western resolution of the religious question is being questioned by the rise of religion in public life in many parts of the world, the Western world included.

This is not the place to analyze the equivocations of this resolution. How recent is the invocation of Christian values to characterize Europe? Why do these values tend to be preferably invoked in situations in which the objective is to demonize Islam or to prevent Turkey from joining the European Union? What are the chosen and the rejected values? (What, exactly, are Christian values?) How relevant is the distance between the terms of the resolution and its practice (the continuing "interference" of religion in family law, reproductive rights, and public education)? How to conceptualize the complex interpenetration of the public and private spheres? To what extent are the eschatological flights of this world the escape from otherwise intolerable social and political injustices and exclusions? And—the greatest equivocation of all—has institutional Christianity (especially the Catholic Church) indeed accepted or merely tolerated such a resolution of the religious question?[5] What is important, rather, is to insist that, without the distinction between the public sphere and the private sphere, and without relegating religion to the latter, the principles of modern Western social regulation and social emancipation are not thinkable at all. The same is true of eighteenth-century natural rights and their successors: from modern constitutionalism to UN human rights declarations.

The modern Western resolution of the religious question is a globalized localism,[6] that is, a local solution that, by virtue of the economic, political, and cultural power of its promoter, ends up extending its range to the entire globe. Western capitalist modernity generated many such globalized localisms, and the resolution of the religious question is probably the most fragile of all. In the colonial territories to which it was transplanted, the distinction between public and private spheres was strictly confined to the "little Europes," the racialized civil societies freely manipulated by the colonial power, scattered throughout Asia, Africa, and the Americas (Said, 1978: 80). No wonder, once historical colonialism came to an end, the distinction between public and private sphere was often considered a foreign imposition both politically and culturally.

A typology of political theologies

I am not concerned here with the religious experience of individuals or communities, but with the way in which such experience is conceived of by religious agents and institutions. I designate as political theology the different modes of conceiving the intervention of religion, as divine message, in the social and po-

litical organization of society. Within Christianity, there is a long historical debate on the nature of political theology (Arjomand, 1993; Scott and Cavanaugh,
2004). In Germany, the debate around it in the 1920s and 1930s was particularly intense, involving many participants, the best known being Carl Schmitt
(1922). Historically, political theology has been identified with a theological
metaphysics that gave religious sanction to existing social and political structures. After the Enlightenment and the social and political processes that led
to the privatization of the individual, conventional theology took the specific
subject created by the Enlightenment as a general subject—humankind—and
grounded thereon the illusion of its apolitical character. In the 1960s, a new political theology emerged, a critical theology, aimed at questioning the existing
social order and the Enlightenment's conception of the individual upon which
it is founded. Far from being a universal subject, such an individual is, in fact, a
middle-class male individual (I would add, white). This criticism underlies the
conception of political theology put forward by, among others, Johann Metz
(1968, 1980), Jürgen Moltmann (1967, 1982), and Dorothee Soelle (1974), as
well as by liberation theologians in Latin America and elsewhere, such as Gustavo Gutiérrez (1971, 2004), Leonardo Boff (1973, 1986, 1997), Clodóvis Boff
(1978, 1984, 1998), Enrique Dussel (1999, 2006), Hugo Assmann and Franz Josef Hinkelammert (1989), Ignacio Ellacuría (1990), Jon Sobrino (1984, 2007),
and Jung Mo Sung (2007, 2011b).[7]

In a more or less radical manner, political theologies question the modern
distinction between the public and the private. The *range* and *criterion or orientation of the intervention* ground some of the fundamental distinctions to
be made among different political theologies. The elaboration of categorical
classifications is always susceptible to the trap of extending to a general group
characteristics that adequately fit only one given subgroup. I am aware that I,
too, may be falling into this trap. For instance, these classifications are probably
more adequate to religions that demand universal acceptance, and thus invest
in heresy, persecution, and excommunication to guarantee the reproduction of
such an acceptance. In this sense, the classifications will apply more easily to
the Semitic religions: Judaism, Christianity, and Islam.[8]

Pluralist and fundamentalist theologies

As to range, a distinction must be made between pluralist and fundamentalist
theologies, of which there are different versions both in Christianity and Islam.
In recent times, in the West, the terms "fundamentalist" and "fundamentalism"

became highly charged with Islamophobic connotations.[9] These biases, incessantly fed by corporate media and extreme right-wing politics (on the rise in Europe), not only distort the real diverse life of Islam in the world but also produce the invisibility of Jewish or Christian fundamentalisms. The latter, in particular, has become a worldwide phenomenon present in such diverse countries as the USA, New Zealand, Australia, or Uganda and Nigeria.[10]

Actually, the origin of the concepts "fundamentalism" and "fundamentalist" is not Islamic, but rather Christian, and more precisely Protestant and North American.[11] As a matter of fact, fundamentalism emerged in the USA at the beginning of the twentieth century. In a brief introduction to this topic, Ruthven (2007: 1) recalls the following words of the journalist H. L. Mencken, written in the 1920s: "Heave an egg out of a Pullman window and you will hit a Fundamentalist almost anywhere in the United States today."[12] Fundamentalism emerged in Southern California at the beginning of the last century and was first spread by a religious publication in several volumes, entitled "The Fundamentals: A Testimony to Truth" (1910–1915). Written by a group of evangelical Protestants of different denominations, the various essays

> aimed at stopping the erosion of what the brothers and their editors considered to be the fundamental beliefs of Protestant Christianity: the inerrancy of the Bible; the direct creation of the world, and humanity, ex nihilo by God (in contrast to Darwinian evolution); the authenticity of miracles; the virgin birth of Jesus, his Crucifixion and bodily resurrection; the substitutionary atonement (the doctrine that Christ died to redeem the sins of humanity); and his imminent return to judge and rule over the world. (Ruthven 2007: 7)

This movement's target was mainly the theory of evolution and its teaching in schools.[13] Borges (2010: 76)[14] sums up fundamentalism in general as a way of thinking based on "a given conception of truth that is confused with the possession of the Fundament." Almond, Appleby, and Sivan, in turn, had already offered the following definition of fundamentalism: "[I]t refers to a discernible pattern of religious militancy by which self-styled 'true believers' attempt to arrest the erosion of religious identity, fortify the borders of the religious community, and create viable alternatives to secular institutions and behaviors" (2003: 17). I will therefore use the terms "fundamentalisms" and "fundamentalist" to refer to theologies—both Christian and Islamic—according to which revelation is conceived of as the all-encompassing principle of organization of society in all its dimensions. In both cases, revelation is usually linked to scripturalism, which means that the organization of social and political life follows a literal interpretation of the sacred books whenever they exist. According to fundamentalist theologies, revelation is an eternal, uncreated divine speech and, as such, human interpretation cannot but be a sacrilegious reduction. Pluralist theologies are theologies that conceive religion as contributing to public life and to the political organization of society but accept the autonomy of both. They manage the tension between reason and revelation by striking a balance between the two. However divine and incommensurable with human reason, revelation's sole purpose is to be accessible to human reason and to be fulfilled through human action in history. This would be impossible if humans were incapable of creative thinking and autonomous action. In sum, pluralist theologies point to a humanistic conception of religion.[15]

Two major issues account for the distinction between pluralist and fundamentalist theologies: the relation between reason and revelation, and the relation between revelation and history. According to Moosa, with reference to one of the leading scholars of Islam in the twentieth century, Fazlur Rahman, one may define the first issue as a tension that "lies in the fact that revelation emanated from a divine and transcendental source but occurs within history and is understood by the human mind" (2000: 13). Rudolf Bultmann, in turn, in a seminal work on the need to reconcile faith and reason, wrote: "[I]t is impossible to repristinate a past world picture by sheer resolve, especially a *mythical* world picture, now that all of our thinking is irrevocably formed by science. A blind acceptance of New Testament mythology would be simply arbitrariness; to make such acceptance a demand of faith would be to reduce faith to a work . . . one would have thought, once and for all" (1984: 3).

The issue of the relation between revelation and history is well formulated by Rahman when he asks, in Moosa's terms: "How do the norms and values of revelation have an enduring relevance to religious communities without becoming anachronistic?" (2000: 15). According to pluralist theologies, revelation occurred in a given social and political context and its relevance is due to the fact that it responds to the existential and social needs of a given time; in sum: a religion *in* history. According to fundamentalist theologies, on the contrary, revelation, being eternal, is acontextual and thus contains in itself and foresees all possible historical needs as well as all the accidents that give rise to them. In sum, history *inside* religion.

Pluralist Christian theologies, while accepting the separation of state and civil society, refuse the state's monopoly on social organization and the notion of civil society as a private sphere. On the contrary, they argue that civil society configures a nonstate public space in which religion must intervene—through the family, civil society institutions, nongovernmental organizations—with the aim of exerting some influence over the state. Opposed to this pluralist political theology, considered to be dominant in Christianity, there has been emerging in recent years a new fundamentalist or integrist[16] political theology according to which the only legitimate community, the only true polity, is the Augustinian city of God in which the invisible and the visible church—centered on the sacraments and hierarchy—takes part. Drawing on the followers of this theology (John Milbank, Stanley Hauerwas, and Oliver O'Donovan, among others), Daniel M. Bell, Jr., asserts that to say the church is the exemplary form of human community "is first and foremost a claim that the meaning of all politics and every community flows from participation in Christ" (2004: 435). Unlike pluralist political theologies, emergent integrist political theologies do not acknowledge the state as an agent of history. According to them, only God is active in history, a conviction, announces Bell, Jr., "now bringing about a new age." Here is his rhetorical question: "What is the proper political correlate of the Christian mythos? Leviathan or the Body of Christ?" (2004: 437).

In Islam, plurality seems to have less to do with the autonomy of the social fields than with the recognition of diversity inside the unity that encompasses all of them. Islamic fundamentalist theologies, on the contrary, do not recognize such diversity or reduce it to a minimum. They conceive religion as the only source of legitimation of political power and maintain, therefore, the unity of religion and the state, under the aegis of religion. According to Achcar, "All brands of Islamic fundamentalism share a common dedication to what is basically a 'medieval-reactionary utopia,' i.e. an imaginary and mythical project of society that is not turned toward the future but toward the medieval past. All of them seek to re-establish on earth the mythicized society and state of early Islamic history" (2008: 66). The fundamental contestation of the modern state often has its expression in the idealization of remote pasts: the medieval, premodern state, in the case of Christian theologies, or the caliphate, in the case of Islamic theologies.[17]

The way I have just characterized fundamentalist theologies may lead to the conclusion that they are essentially antimodern. But this may be too rash a conclusion, particularly considering the rise of fundamentalisms for the past decades, whether in Judaism, Christianity, or Islam. As a matter of fact, it is amazing how easily different fundamentalisms, while trying to uphold the identity of their own religious communities, cross institutional and cultural borders and successfully reproduce practices and rituals in the most diverse contexts. They are indeed transnational movements that efficaciously utilize every type of organization, communication, formation, and commercialization that global capitalism has provided. This is what leads Lehmann to assert that fundamentalist movements are "a quintessentially modern phenomenon," even if engaging in a different kind of globalization than the one usually associated with cosmopolitanism (1998: 630). Steve Bruce, in turn, although stressing that some dimensions of modernity (science and technology as well as political and cultural pluralism) do set limits on fundamentalist expansion, insists, having particularly in mind Protestant fundamentalism in the United States, that the latter "does seem to challenge the assumption that one cannot believe God actually made the world in six days, that the Bible is the inspired (and even dictated) Word of God and that the Second Coming is imminent while living in a city making use of state of the art technology" (1990: 487). The relation of fundamentalisms, whether religious or nonreligious, with modernity and, above all, with the acceleration of globalization can still be conceived of as a dialectical relation.[18] As Nagata says, "It may be no coincidence that funda-mentalism has been added to the academic and public lexicon at a time when the global (dis)order, with its attendant transnationalism, cosmopolitanism, pluralisms, relativisms, and movement of people and ideas across the world has contributed to an obsessive concern with identity, authenticity, and ultimate values—the fundamentals of existence" (2001: 482). The rise of fundamen-talisms requires a more complex analysis of what is meant by modernity, an analysis similar to the one that in the 1950s and 1960s looked into Nazism and considered it an integral part of modernity, rather than its opposite. I will come back to this issue below when I study the affinities between fundamentalisms and neoliberal globalization.

Traditionalist and progressive theologies

As regards the criterion or orientation of the religious intervention, one can dis-tinguish traditionalist[19] and progressive theologies. As in the case of pluralist and fundamentalist theologies, there are different Christian and Islamic versions.

Traditionalist theologies intervene in political society by defending, as the best solution for the present, the social and political arrangements of the past. They make use of theological data in order to emphasize political ideas that trace political authority back to religious authority with the aim of giving politics the stability and immunity possessed by religion. According to Moosa, traditionalisms of different stripes consist in a promise

> to reconnect contemporary Muslim societies with their glorious past. They have one precondition: Our understanding of Islam must be completely stripped of all its historical and cultural accretions; all past interpretations and elaborations are to be eschewed. The credo of this group is to return to the Qur'an, and for some, to engage with a sliver of the authentic prophetic tradition, that will incredulously lead to the recovery of a "true" Islam. (2008: 568)

In Christianity, a traditionalist theology means, for example, that the distinction between the religion of the oppressed and the religion of the oppressors is not acknowledged. What from another perspective is viewed as the religion of the oppressor—a bourgeois, spiritualist religion, without a critical position vis-à-vis structural injustices (Metz, 1980)—is said to be the standard and legitimate religious experience, while the religion of the oppressed is either stigmatized or ignored. The thinking of Joseph Ratzinger, Pope Benedict XVI (now Pope Emeritus), is an example of the rejection of the theological centrality of the experience of the oppressed, or, more generally, of orthopraxis (right living or practice instead of right doctrine or orthodoxy). Indeed, according to Ratzinger, this kind of theological centrality replaces truth by practice and, as such, displaces the axis of religion, reducing the ideal of a better society to the domain of the "profane-utopian" (2007: 68).

Christian progressive theologies, on the contrary, are grounded on the distinction between the religion of the oppressed and the religion of the oppressors, and severely criticize institutional religion as a religion of the oppressors. Since, according to them, it is not legitimate to separate the analysis of religion from the analysis of the relations of production, the religion of the oppressors is, in Western modernity, a "religion of capitalism," and I would add, of colonialism and patriarchy. In the case of liberation theologies, the critique of capitalism and its "idolatry of the market" (Assmann and Hinkelammert, 1989; Sung, 2011a), much influenced by Marxism, particularly in its Latin American version, is at the core of a theological renewal that focuses on the poor and oppressed as a collective entity. As Libânio states:

> The assumption of this reflection is that economic theories have not only ethical but also theological implications. Explicit or implicit theologies underlie economic theories and end up legitimating the latter, enveloping them in an aura of "economic religion." Actually, capitalism's goal is to go to the depths of the

human heart and unveil the mystery of its desire, which is ultimately the mystery of religion. This "economic religion" creates the "transcendental illusion" of the fulfillment here on earth of every human desire by means of consumerism and hedonism.[20] (1999)

Liberation theology conceives of faith as being liberating only to the extent that it contributes to the structural and collective liberation of the poor. The poor are both the object of theology (its main concern) and its subject (as they are the protagonists of history and its interpretation), and they constitute as well the social ground on the basis of which theology must be enunciated. Liberation theology constitutes, in itself, a constellation of theologies wherein the category of "the poor" unfolds contextually to include the victims of capitalism and the peoples oppressed by the colonial and postcolonial powers (in Latin America, indigenous peoples and Afro-descendents), as well as the "melting pot" resulting from the encounters, but also the violations of cultures and bodies (Gonzalez, 2004).

These theologies have been opening up increasingly not only to an ecumenical but also to an interreligious perspective. Two main reasons account for this. On the one hand, theology's center of gravity has moved to the Global South, not only for demographic reasons but also because the winds of the most creative theologies are now blowing from there. On the other hand, the global dimension of the problems challenging humanity today requires responses on a global scale as well, which only interreligious dialogues and theologies can provide. Such theologies are, nonetheless, critical of global projects aiming at new forms of religious power over the public space. As Tamayo says: "Liberation needs every religion and every culture in order to be complete. The marriage bringing together liberation, cultures, and religions is not a marriage 'for powers'" (2005: 12). The project of intercultural theology defended both by this author and by Fornet-Betancourt (2006)[21] is centered around the axis of an intercultural liberation theology and a critique of the current epistemological asymmetry resulting from neoliberal globalization and from the model of Western scientific and technical knowledge. Its proposal consists of a dialogue among contextualized critical movements:

What this means, however, is that we must bring this critical work to bear on the social, political, and cultural movements of every woman and man fighting for the recognition of their difference, since without such a moment of rebellion there is no critique. These are the movements showing, if I may resort to symbolism from Christian theology, that the "resurrection of the flesh" is possible, that is to say, that the situational contextualities, charged with history and life, erupt in the course of the world and imprint on it many faces and rhythms. (Fornet-Betancourt, 2006: 15)[22]

According to progressive Christian theologies, the separation of public and private space has always been a way of domesticating or neutralizing the emancipatory potential of religion, a process that has counted on the complicity and even active participation of conservative theologies.[23] According to Metz (1980: 63), while accepting the idea of the privatized individual (a white male individual, I would add), theology established a contrast between the subject, on the one hand, and history and society, on the other, and with it lost any base for solidarity and hope. On the contrary, for a politically progressive theology, "the faith of Christians is a praxis in history and society" (Metz, 1980: 73). In a similar vein, Soelle asserts that the aim of political theology is "to bring faith and action together more satisfactorily" (1974: 2). Progressive Christian theologies insist mainly on the history of the sociological movement generated by Jesus.[24] According to them, this movement shows that religion does not emerge from the private domain. For good or ill, religion never left the public domain: for ill, because it was an essential legitimating element of colonial or imperial order; for good, because it has always been an inspiring source for the social groups and movements that have struggled against injustice and oppression throughout history. As regards postcolonial theologies, a specific version of progressive theologies, faith must be considered, on the one hand, as a critique of political imperialism reiterated by the imperial forms of Christianity and, on the other hand, as a positive engagement with the hybridity of between-spaces.

> The task of a postcolonial theology will not be to shore up the barriers between the Christian and non-Christian, the holy and the profane, the church and the world, the ethical and the immoral, even the Creator and the creation. Nor will it be simply to demolish them. We will want instead to pay careful attention to what happens in all these in-between places. What refuses enclosure? What crosses over? What revels and reveals itself in the many tongues of many peoples? What is dis/closed in the shifting borderlands? (Keller, Nausner, and Rivera, 2004: 14)[25]

Some progressive Islamic theologies, of which Ali Shariati (1980, 1986) is a remarkable example, likewise address radical criticisms of capitalism and the West (and, in his case, of Marxism as well), arguing that they have been a source of dehumanization and exploitation. Shariati thought that, at the dawn of a new, postcapitalist and postcommunist era, the human being would find a new way of salvation in which Islam would play a fundamental role, both because it offers a spiritual interpretation of the universe and because it constitutes a new humanism. But to play such a role, Islam would have to free itself from the effects of centuries of stagnation, superstition, and contamination, and to be put forth as a living ideology. In turn, Dabashi (2008) considers that Islamic liberation theology would require liberation from Western imperialism and a cosmopolitan openness in dialogue with the various cultures. In both their Christian and Islamic versions, progressive theologies also assume a particularly relevant formulation in feminist theologies. These theologies are very critical of associating religion and its hierarchical structures with the patriarchal order, and of legitimating patriarchy and the submission of women; they reconstruct theology and the way the foundational texts are read on the basis of the emancipatory experiences of women inside the religions.[26]

Distinguishing between different kinds of theology (pluralist and fundamentalist; progressive and traditionalist) shows that the relations among the rising political theologies, forms of globalization, and human rights are not univocal or monolithic. As regards globalization, all of them are nonhegemonic to the extent that they question either the all-encompassing efficacy of secular institutions or the secular nature of the struggles against it. However, progressive theologies carry a strong counterhegemonic potential. Ulrich Duchrow, for instance, raises the issue of the need for a theology capable of helping to "construct an interdisciplinary theoretical work on alternatives to a neoliberal hegemony" (2006: 203). Indeed, many of the religious social movements that have taken part in the World Social Forum are inspired by progressive theologies, liberation theologies in particular.[27] On the other hand, traditionalist theologies, to the extent that they inform the processes of religious globalization, are nonhegemonic forms of globalization, but in no way are they counterhegemonic in the sense used here.

Chapter 3

The Case of Islamic Fundamentalism

NON-WESTERN (and non-Christian) political theologies, particularly when they are militantly anti-Western, pose specific challenges to the distinctions and categorizations made in the previous chapter.[1] What does it mean to be anti-Western? Does it mean the rejection of Western modernity as a cultural project or the rejection of colonialism and capitalism? For instance, although the Muslim Brotherhood in Egypt—which is far from being a monolithic movement (Saadawi and Hetata, 1999)—is viewed and views itself as anti-Western, the relations of some of its members with Western capitalism, including with its most predatory financial features, are well known. Hassan al-Banna, founder of the Muslim Brotherhood (1924), claimed that ideas and institutions in Islamic societies should come from Islam and not from the West. He admitted importation from the West in the following areas: administrative systems; applied sciences; communications; services; hospitals and pharmacies; industry, animal husbandry, and agriculture; nuclear energy for peaceful purposes; urban planning, construction, housing, and traffic flow; energy. "Apart from this we do not need anything. Islam includes all things" (Saadawi and Hetata, 1999: 5).[2] On the political level, what to think of Islamic organizations in Egypt, Tunisia, Algeria, Lebanon, Palestine, or Indonesia participating in and sometimes winning electoral processes framed by Western-based conceptions of liberal democracy? What about the Islamic Republic of Iran being based on a popular revolution followed by parliamentary democracy? And in the case of fair and free electoral victories by Islamic parties, is it equally Western for Western capitalist powers to accept them when convenient (Turkey, 2002) and to refuse or boycott them when inconvenient (Algeria, 1991, and Palestine, 2006)? On the other hand, does being anti-Western preclude the possibility of entering into tactical alliances with Western political powers, having particularly in mind the case of the Taliban in Afghanistan in the 1980s being trained in Pakistan and armed by the USA to fight the (then) USSR (Achcar, 2006)?

Aside from the obvious political issues, these questions raise conceptual problems for which there are no consensual, let alone univocal, solutions. Dealing with political theologies has precisely the distinct merit of revealing the limits of the theoretical work in this domain. I will illustrate this in this chapter by analyzing the globalization of Islam and of some forms of Islamic political theology. This is a minefield in which claims of conceptual difficulty are often mixed with implicit or even explicit assumptions about real or imagined political threats. Indeed, I think it is unwarranted to make general evaluations of political threat or the dangerousness of different versions of fundamentalism, be it Jewish fundamentalism, Christian fundamentalism (more on this below), combinations of both, as in the case of Christian Zionism,[3] or Islamic fundamentalism. In this chapter I focus on fundamentalist Islam, nowadays a highly visible current within Islamic religion. But in no way should it be forgotten that there is an immense diversity of religious experiences inside Islam.[4] The power of fundamentalist Islam has its own causes, some of which I analyze in this book, but it is highly amplified by its visibility in the Western media and the latter's obsession with the "war on terror."[5] An analysis of Islam in Africa, in Indonesia, with the largest Islamic population in the world, or even in Europe, provides us with a much richer picture of Islamic experiences.[6] In general, according to fundamentalist Islam, on the basis of a supposedly rigid interpretation of the *sharia*, religion permeates the whole of society and the personal lives of all believers. When I refer to a rigid interpretation of the *sharia*, I do not mean a static interpretation of it, nor the idea that there cannot be a plurality of rigid interpretations. Talal Asad calls our attention to the need to overcome the orientalist thesis, "propounded in the West since at least the beginning of the twentieth century, that the Islamic legal tradition became static—that 'the gates of *ijtihad* were closed,' as the famous phrase has it—after the first formative centuries." According to Asad, "change was always important to the *sharia*, and its flexibility was retained through such technical devices as *'urf* (custom), *maslaha* (public interest), and *darura* (necessity)" (2003: 221). Margot Badran also appeals to the distinction between "the *sharia* as the path discerned from the Qur'an that Muslims are exhorted to follow in life (*sharia* as divine inspiration and guiding principles) and so-called '*sharia* law(s)' (laws deriving from understandings of *fiqh* that are man-made, and therefore open to questioning and change)." According to Badran, "The *shari'a*, as 'the path indicated in the scripture as the word of God, is sacred; but it needs to be ascertained through human effort" (2009: 285). Again, according to Moosa: "Literally *shari'a* means 'the trodden path.' Muslims understand that Moses had a *shari'a*, just as Jesus and countless other prophets had an equivalent of the *shari'a* as [their] moral point of reference" (2008: 570).[7]

By resorting to Islam's cultural and historical legacy and engaging in a radical critique of Western imperialism, fundamentalist Islam proposes to change the living conditions of the believers who were defrauded by the failure of the national and pro-Western development projects of the states ruling over Muslim populations in the first four decades of the twentieth century. Whereas the more extremist tendencies focus on violent criticisms and deeds against what is considered to be Western interests, the more moderate tendencies engage in appealing to voluntary work in education, health, and social welfare, in what amounts to something like an Islamic modernization project (Westerlund and Svanberg, 1999: 20). On the basis of criteria such as these, the well-known leftist Egyptian writer, Sherif Hetata, says about the Muslim Brotherhood in Egypt:

> If we consider as fundamentalists those people that have a narrow, orthodox, fanatical doctrinaire interpretation of Islam, then they are a minority. They are a very active minority. They are sometimes a powerful minority. But in Egypt . . . I don't think the really fundamentalist movements include the Moslem Brothers. I am not sympathetic to the Moslem Brothers, in particular to their leadership . . . you cannot have progress in a country like Egypt if you do not deal with Islam, if you do not give an enlightened interpretation of Islam. Islam is the life of the people, it is our tradition and our cultural heritage. We must work with the Moslem Brothers, but not with their leadership" (1989: 23–25).[8]

Fundamentalist Islam is definitely part of a larger process, which I call here the globalization of political theologies. I am aware that the notion of political theology applied to Islam, as in "political Islam," is a minefield that has been used in recent (and not-so-recent) years to demonize Islam and to reinforce the century-old orientalist view that Muslim societies, besides being retrograde, nondemocratic, and violent, are monolithic in terms of their belief systems. Two of the most insightful critical analyses of this phenomenon are Modood (2003) and Sayyid (2005, 2014). I fully share their concerns and also subscribe to the cautionary note proposed by Sadowsky that the analysis of political Islam should not obscure the following facts: Muslim societies tend to be at least as diverse as they are similar; there is a large gap between Islamic doctrine and Muslim practice; the aspirations of Muslims do not differ markedly from those of other cultures, although the means they deploy to pursue them may differ; despite the criticisms made during the Enlightenment, religion neither prevents people from behaving rationally nor from innovating; the great struggles in which Muslims are caught are structured by history but not determined by it. Their outcomes may still be uncertain (2006: 234). It goes without saying that this applies as well to Hindu, Jewish, or Christian societies. The political and intellectual difference, of course, is that today there is much more talk about political Islam than about political Hinduism, political Judaism, or political Christianity.[9]

Fundamentalist Islam operates outside the boundaries of Islamic nationalism and feeds on its crisis.[10] Islamic nationalism was, in fact, a factor of national political projects that emerged from the struggle against colonialism. These projects translated themselves into authoritarian states, some of them revolutionary, some of them traditionalist. All of them, however, were intent on instrumentalizing or controlling Islam under the pretense of modernizing it and putting it at the service of the state. If the traditionalists found in Islam the glorious past that ratified them, the revolutionaries used Islam to give the future back to Islamic societies. In either case, the question was one of authoritarian legitimation processes, in which personalistic political power frequently resorted to religious references, in spite of alleged laicity and secularism. We should not forget that in Muslim societies the modern experience of secularism is also an experience of dictatorship. This means that the democratic value attributed to secularism in the Global North is absent in or cannot be transposed mechanically to the Global South.[11]

The fundamentalist political Islam of today feeds on the failure of these projects; rather than state-centric, it is society-centric and global in scope. It transfers the project of renovation to the transnational society of believers, subjecting the state to a radical critique and accusing it of complicity with or submission to Western imperialism.[12] The latter is the major enemy in that it has been the basic source of humiliation for the Islamic peoples. While some versions radically oppose all the constitutive dimensions of hegemonic, neoliberal globalization—economic, social, political, and cultural—others distinguish among them and, while refusing the cultural and political dimensions, embrace the economic one.

The most extremist versions of Islamic fundamentalist theologies[13] have very little to do with counterhegemonic globalization as it was defined above and as it emerges, for instance, from within the process of the World Social Forum (WSF).[14] The counterhegemonic globalization of the WSF welcomes and celebrates cultural and political diversity; it is secular, even if it includes religion-inspired movements, which in any case must respect the large majority of nonreligious movements;[15] the project of the future society that it defends is open, since the designation of "another world is possible" includes many forms of social emancipation; it utilizes very fluid, horizontal organizational models, with no central leadership, and whose fulfillment depends on voluntary convergences; lastly, while proposing a new politics and a new epistemology, many of the movements it embraces share the cultural, philosophical, and ethical paradigms of Western modernity. Regarding many of these aspects, the globalization of fundamentalist political Islam is at the antipodes of the counterhegemonic globalization of the WSF.[16] Intriguingly enough, it seems rather to share some similarities both with modernist utopias, which were closed models of a future society, and with some characteristics of hegemonic neoliberal globalization: unique thought (whether neoliberalism or Islamism), juridical ecumene (be it the rule of law or the *Shari'a*), monolithic expansionism (be it the market or conversion), and the critique of the state (be it the welfare state or the secular state).

A specific reference is in order here regarding the relations between, on the one hand, Islam, and particularly fundamentalist Islam, and, on the other, women's rights, the struggle against sexual discrimination, and feminism. This may well be the field in which it is most important to counter the monolithic conceptions of Islam prevalent in the West today. The struggles against global capitalism and in favor of counterhegemonic globalization must take into account the different forms of power and oppression feeding the reproduction of inequality and discrimination—class, gender, race, caste, sexual orientation, religious choice—and fight against them all. In the context of Islam, and particularly in the context of fundamentalist Islam, the struggle against sexual discrimination appears to be one of the most difficult. In this regard, Western modernity and Islam seem to be far apart. So much so that one of the positions supporting women's rights in Islam takes off from the fundamental opposition between Islam and Western modernity, while drawing predominantly on the latter.[17] The debate concerning the compatibility or incompatibility between Islam and women's liberation has divided the feminist movement. The compatibility thesis is based on the idea of Islamic feminism, that it is possible to create, in Islam itself, an emancipatory alternative to secular feminism or an approach compatible with it. This idea is based on experiences warranted by Islamic women of pluralist and progressive theological orientations, often designated as Islamic reformism.[18] Margot Badran, for example, maintains that Islamic feminism "transcends and eradicates old binaries. These include polarities between 'religious' and 'secular' and between 'East' and 'West.'" She adds: "I stress this because not infrequently there are those who see Islamic feminism as setting up or reconfirming dichotomies. . . . I have argued that Islamic feminist discourse . . . closes gaps and reveals common concerns and goals, starting with the basic affirmation of gender equality and social justice" (2009: 245).

Islamic feminism builds upon the experiences of women in countries where fundamentalist Islam provides the framework for the struggle for legal reform or interpretations of the *sharī'a* capable of granting full citizenship to women.[19] Such interpretations are frequently based on a return to the Qur'an as the critical instance of "human" *(fiqh)* interpretations of *sharī'a*. Here is Mir-Hosseini's comment in this regard:

> I contend that patriarchal interpretations of the *sharī'a* can and must be challenged at the level of *fiqh*, which is nothing more than the human understanding of the divine will, that is, what we are able to understand of the *sharī'a* in this world at the legal level. In other words, *sharī'a* is the transcendental ideal that embodies the justice of Islam and the spirit of the Koranic revelations. This transcendental ideal, which condemns all relations of exploitation and domination, underpins Muslim women's quest and the critique of patriarchal constructions of gender relations, which are to be found not only in the vast corpus of jurisprudential texts but also in the positive laws that are claimed to be rooted in the sacred texts. (2006: 633)

The incompatibility thesis, in turn, purports to be grounded not so much on normative ideals as on empirical evidence about the actual patterns of gender relations and the interpretations of the *sharī'a* that prevail in societies dominated by fundamentalist Islam. According to some authors, "Islamic feminism" is an oxymoron, a contradiction in terms. "If by feminism is meant easing patriarchal pressures on women, making patriarchy less appalling, 'Islamic feminism' is certainly a feminist trend. But if feminism is a movement to abolish patriarchy, to contribute toward a society in which individuals can fashion their lives free from economic, political, social, and cultural constraints, then

'Islamic feminism' proves considerably inadequate because it can never challenge the traditional, patriarchal system" (Mojab, 2001: 131).

There is a third way of pondering the relation between Islam and the rights of women; it consists in the xenophobic recourse to discourses of antagonism between the two as a form of Islamophobia, that is to say, as a place of enunciation of what is truly considered antagonistic: Islam and the West. The polemics over banning the veil in several European countries is a good example of this sham "feminism," in the end Islamophobic, that some feminists have adopted as well.[20] It is highly probable that this topic will continue to divide the movements of Islamic women from those of their non-Islamic allies. One of the most productive facets of the debate and the political struggle is, to my mind, a critical feminism attempting to include in the same analytical horizon the limitations of not only Islamic feminism but also Western, liberal feminism. Indeed, both conceptions of feminism lack a critique of the mechanisms that reproduce unequal power relations, and that is why the real inequalities between men and women are devalued under the legal fetishism of formal equality. Thus, critical feminism renders the relation between Islam and Western modernity far more complex.

Chapter 4

The Case of Christian Fundamentalism

IF ISLAMIC FUNDAMENTALISM raises questions regarding its rejection of some features of Western modernity—its static interpretation of the *shari'a* (as divine law); its incompatibility with democratic regimes and the rights of women—the same is true, albeit in a different way, of Christian fundamentalism, especially in its Protestant strain.[1] Though flourishing in other parts of the world (Latin America, Africa, and Asia), a specific reference to Christian fundamentalism and political theology, in general, in the United States is justified for two reasons. On the one side, as Michel Perry affirms, "the citizenry of the United States is one of the most religious—perhaps even the most religious—citizenries of the world's advanced industrial democracies" (1997: 3). On the other side, the American brands of Christian fundamentalism have been the most globalized, offering themselves to multiple vernacularizations or adaptations according to the contexts in which they operate.

Christian fundamentalism reemerged in the 1980s in the United States and became known as the New Christian Right. One of the main mentors of the New Christian Right was the Baptist pastor Jerry Falwell (1980). His Moral Majority Inc. and similar organizations, such as Christian Voice, Religious Roundtable, and American Coalition for Traditional Values, became pressure groups campaigning on a whole range of public policy issues, such as abortion, homosexuality, the teaching of evolution in school, the threat of "secular humanism," minority rights legislation, and prayer in public schools (Bruce, 1990: 479).[2] According to Casanova, the dominant tendency of fundamentalist Protestantism is its aim to (re)establish "the cultural hegemony of evangelical Protestantism [in order to] re-Christianize the Constitution, the republic, and American civil society" (1994: 159). The argument of these fundamentalist movements is that modern society liberalized the family, education, and abortion, which they consider a betrayal of Christian values. They argue for less state intervention in the private sphere: "We advocate the passage of family protection legislation which would counteract disruptive federal intervention into family life and encourage the restoration of family unity, parental authority, and a climate of traditional authority . . . and reinforce traditional husband-and-wife relationships" (Falwell, 1980: 136). Fundamentalist movements also maintain that the issues that emancipatory movements, namely those concerning women and gays and lesbians, have managed to introduce into the public sphere should be considered again as part of the private sphere. Here is Falwell: "We must stand against the Equal Rights Amendment, the feminist revolution, and the homosexual revolution" (1980: 19). At the same time, they fight for the Christianization of state structures such as those of education: "It is the Christian school movement and the restoration of voluntary prayer in public schools that will provide the most important means of educating our children in the concepts of patriotism and morality" (Falwell, 1980: 223). According to the New Right, the American way of life must identify itself "once again" with God's law: "Right living must be re-established as an American way of life. . . . The authority of Bible morality must once again be recognized as the legitimate guiding principle of our nation" (1980: 265). In 1984, Richard Viguerie, one of the leading figures of the New Christian Right, asserted: "Conservatives should work for the day when the November contest is between a conservative Democrat and a conservative Republican. Then we can go fishing or play golf on election day knowing that it doesn't matter if a Republican or a Democrat wins." (Bruce, 1990: 479). Thirty years later this statement sounds like a fulfilled prophecy.

From the New Right standpoint, the re-Christianization of American society implies as well an articulation between what they consider the Christian ethics of responsibility and market economy. Gary North, president of the Institute for Christian Economics in Tyler (Texas), presents the objectives of the Institute: "The ICE is dedicated to the proposition that biblical ethics requires full personal responsibility, and this responsible human action flourishes most productively within a framework of limited government, political decentralization, and minimum interference with the economy by the civil government."[3] North observes that the most vocal comments of the past fifty years were those in favor of social Christianity, which, he maintains, is "outspokenly pro-government intervention." In his (clearly theocratic) opinion,[4] conservative Christians keep silent

> because they have convinced themselves that any policy statement of any sort
> regarding social and economic life is always illegitimate. In short, there is no
> such thing as a correct, valid policy statement that a church or denomination
> can make. The results of this opinion have been universally devastating . . . . The
> public is convinced that to speak out on social matters in the name of Christ is
> to be radical. *Christians are losing by default.* (North, n.d.)

Furthermore, according to North, the "wealth formula" for a society's economic growth consists in following the Mosaic Law:

> Moses delivered to Israel the judicial foundation of long-term economic growth.
> Through God's grace, the nation could adhere to the Mosaic law. This would
> have produced the growth in population and per capita wealth promised by
> Moses. But God, in His sovereignty, did not enable Israel to obey. The opportu
> nity was lost. But this does not mean that the potential for enormous long-term
> growth was not available to Israel. Had Israel continued to grow as fast as the
> world's population has grown since 1776, the filling of the earth would have
> been completed millennia ago. But it was not God's time. The rate of population
> growth will vary until such time as God has determined that time must end. We
> will run out of time before we run out of raw materials, space, and productive
> new ideas. Time is the crucial limit to growth, not nature. (North, 1997)

Theology of prosperity (gospel of prosperity) is another way of legitimating, from the viewpoint of religion, capitalist economies and the social inequalities derived therefrom; assuming that God wants human beings to be prosperous, the latter, by themselves, are deemed incapable of so becoming, since God is considered the legitimating principle of wealth and enrichment[5]. In this line of thought, Edwene Gaines, for instance, wonders "if it is greedy to desire material goods." He provides his own reply:

> Being rich doesn't mean you're greedy or bad. . . . Greed is when you say, "I want
> this, and I don't want you to have it." It is not greedy to say, "I want lots, and I
> want you to have lots, too." If you believe that there is no end to God's abun
> dance, then everyone should have all that they want, and then more. Money
> is like love: The more you give away, the more you have. Love is a limitless re
> source, and so is money, and both were created by God to enrich our lives and
> allow us to live fully, joyfully, and completely. (2005: 19)

According to this position, the social state is viewed negatively as a sacrilegious attempt to replace God's regulating power and as a way of rendering individuals "lazy," as we learn from Kenneth Hagin:

> In the time of the Early Church, civil governments didn't have any welfare programs. The Church took care of its own needy, including widows and orphans. . . . We've gotten away from this; the government is doing everything; the government is almost God, you see. But Paul said the widows' relatives should take care of them. And he said believers should work with their own hands to earn their living. . . . A man who's living off of other people is really stealing from them. And while I'm on the subject, people who go to a church and don't put anything in—who never pay their tithes or give offerings—are stealing from the rest of the people. They want to get blessed, but they want the other fellow to pay for it. These people need to put off the character of the thief and put on the character of Jesus. He was a giver! (1985: 11-12)

Kyle Murray points out the economic impact of these fundamentalist (charismatic and Pentecostal) movements, also known as "renewalist," having in mind both their reproduction of neoliberal hegemony and their expansion at the global level: "With over 500 million believers worldwide, Renewalism represents one of the fastest-growing faith movements in the planet— particularly among the popular masses in parts of the developing world" (2012: 266). According to Murray, this phenomenon has generated a demographic group with transnational linkages bearing the same worldview and the same forms of activism inside states and between different states, societies, and markets. Not only did renewalist movements structure a global financial market by promoting the circulation of funding from some churches and communities to others at the internal, external, and global levels, but they also created "micro-lending schemes designed to bolster Christian entrepreneurism" as well as "regional, state and global Christian business associations in order to collectively organize Christian business people and exert influence in marketplaces" (Murray, 2012: 270). Furthermore, these movements also influence the labor market directly: "As rural dwellers migrate en masse to new centres of industrial development, particularly in parts of sub-Saharan Africa and Latin America, Renewalist institutions, intellectuals and forces are there waiting to help these migrants make sense of their new existence.[6] They provide migrants with a new conception of the world that gives them an individual 'role' within and between states, societies and markets" (Murray, 2012: 270).

There is also a Catholic theology legitimating capitalism. Although Pope John Paul II, in particular, along with his violent criticisms of Marxism, strongly criticized capitalism, especially on account of its consumerism and materialism, some Catholic authors have been commending capitalism as the system that gives more opportunities to the poor. Michael Novak, highly respected in Catholic schools and programs of economics, is the author of a book—*The Spirit of Democratic Capitalism* (1982)—whose line of argument can be summarized in the author's own words:

> It is easy to understand how the *practical* case for capitalism is easy to grasp. No other system so rapidly raises up the living standards of the poor, so thoroughly improves the conditions of life, or generates greater social wealth and distributes it more broadly. In the long competition of the last 100 years, neither socialist nor third-world experiments have performed as well in improving the lot of common people, paid higher wages, and more broadly multiplied liberties and opportunities.[7]

Globalization of Christian fundamentalism

The expansion of Christian fundamentalist movements throughout the world, whether by means of proselytizing missions or through electronic resources, has significant political impact. As they expand, these movements also become indigenous. In Brazil, for example, Neo-Pentecostalism or the Third Wave of Pentecostalism is a chapter of Evangelicalism that joins together denominations derived from classical Pentecostalism or even traditional Christian churches (Baptist, Methodist, and the like). A good number of these movements possess or utilize media outlets, including TV, radio, periodicals, presses, or Internet portals and sites of their own. Nowadays, with fifty-nine members, the Neo-Pentecostals make up the second-largest group of representatives in the Brazilian National Congress, which explains why in the 2010 general elections the debates focused on the abortion question rather than on the economy, housing, and education; or why Marco Feliciano, a pastor of a Pentecostal denomination (Igreja Evangélica Assembléia de Deus [Assembly of God Evangelical Church]), became the president of the Brazilian Parliament's Commission for Human Rights and proposed a controversial law known as the "gay cure" that, if passed, would permit psychologists to treat homosexuality as an illness.[8]

This situation finds striking similarities in Asia as well as in sub-Saharan Africa. Analyzing the case of the Philippines, Maria Anicia Co stressed the fact that in this country—marked by a majority of people of the Christian faith—many youngsters had left the Catholic Church "in favor of fundamentalist sects." According to Co, this reality resulted from people moving away from the classical doctrine of asceticism and spiritual richness to the prosperity gospel (2013: 5).

In African contexts, the situation is quite different. If early Pentecostalism preached an ascetic doctrine, stressing strict moral ethics and biblical inerrancy, modern Pentecostalism embraces a gospel of accumulation, thus adjusting to and indeed legitimating the neoliberal wave spreading over the continent (Gifford, 2001; Meyer, 2004; Akoko, 2007). However, in view of the profound social and economic crises that shake the African continent, many churches have returned to the interpretation of accumulation as the way of sin, with increasing exhortations to believers to shun all unnecessary (un-African) material and carnal pleasures. Probably the most controversial impact of such exhortations has been the institutionalization of discrimination against homosexuals in various countries. As widely reported, two African countries, Nigeria and Uganda, have recently passed strict antigay legislation.[9] In Uganda, the Anti-Homosexuality Act of 2014 establishes certain homosexual acts punishable with imprisonment for life.[10] Other laws ban "indecent acts or behavior tending to corrupt morals," including the use of miniskirts. In Nigeria, on the other hand, the Same-Sex Marriage Prohibition Act (2013)[11] establishes a prison sentence of up to fourteen years imprisonment for same-sex marriages or civil unions. Any person who is openly gay and anyone who "registers, operates or participates in gay clubs, societies and organizations" can be sentenced to up to ten years in prison. As governmental authorities have emphasized, this law applies also to foreigners who visit Nigeria to help promote LGBT causes.

All these bills claim that being gay is "un-African." Challenging this view, a well-known Nigerian writer, Chimamanda Adichie, wrote:

> [Such a law] shows a failure of our democracy, because the mark of a true democracy is not in the rule of its majority but in the protection of its minority—otherwise mob justice would be considered democratic. The law is also unconstitutional, ambiguous, and a strange priority in a country with so many real problems. Above all else, however, it is unjust. Even if this was not a country of abysmal electricity supply where university graduates are barely literate and people die of easily-treatable causes and Boko Haram commits casual mass murders, this law would still be unjust. We cannot be a just society unless we are able to accommodate benign difference, accept benign difference, live and let

live. We may not understand homosexuality, we may find it personally abhor-
rent but our response cannot be to criminalize it. (Adichie, 2014)

The homophobic attitudes supporting these laws are violent and dangerous. The criminalization of sexual orientation poses serious challenges to
identity politics and violates human rights. Since the bill has been approved
the first gay sex trial is currently (October 2014) under way in Uganda. As the
accusation states, the two indicted males have been charged with engaging
in sex acts "against the order of nature."[12] Uganda's Catholic Archbishop of
Kampala, Cyprian Lwanga, stated in December 2009 that the bill was unnecessary and "at odds with the core values" of Christianity, expressing particular
concerns at the death penalty provisions. But, in line with the abovementioned
proposal advanced in Brazil, Lwanga has defended that homosexuals should
be encouraged to seek rehabilitation.[13]

From a postcolonial perspective it should be emphasized that these countries have passed these laws under the influence of a multilayered set of Western interferences that can be traced back to colonial impositions. In Uganda,
Sylvia Tamale, a well-known feminist scholar, has argued that the roots of cat-
egorization of many practices as "barbaric," such as the case of homosexuality,
lie in colonial times (2009: 52). She further claims that many of the African
"traditional" elements of culture are the result of interpretation and construction, developed upon a strict articulation between colonialists and local patri-
archs. In the same line of argument, Dlamini (2006) maintains that Western
colonization exported homophobia, but not homosexuality, to Africa.

Today, this influence is reproduced and amplified through political alliances developed across the world by conservative and religious circles. As
widely reported, Western conservative Christian movements have supported
and assisted in drafting the abovementioned laws.[14] Behind this support is
the claim that LGBT rights are not human rights. This Western proselytism
by conservative religious groups has spread throughout Africa.[15] Right-wing
evangelists have promoted antigay legislation in Kenya (unsuccessfully) and
Zimbabwe. In the latter case, the new constitution, approved in 2013 by an
overwhelming popular vote, includes a ban on gay marriage. Again, one of the
supporting claims for this ban is the "un-African," "anti-Christian," "immoral"
nature of homosexuality.

The insistence of conservative circles in Uganda to characterize homosexuality as a colonial imposition, while expressing the recognition of the
continuities of the colonial project—the erasure of Africa's history of sexual

diversity—mainly aims at hiding "the neocolonial aspirations of the US religious right to globalize the US culture wars" (Cheney, 2012: 80). The close alignment of state power with religious fundamentalists (Obadare, 2006) has geopolitical implications that reach much beyond religious issues.

In the Global South, the extraordinary spread of Christian fundamentalism is a mass culture phenomenon, rather than a grassroots, folk culture phenomenon. Folk culture, so crucial to liberation theologies, resides in the valorization of the authentic and the autochthonous, indeed, the valorization of what corresponds to a specific identity that is contextualized in time and space. The cultural and life density of such authenticity requires an effort of intercultural translation on the part of the Christian message and messengers so that evangelization does not appear as an act of naked violence. On the contrary, fundamentalist currents, especially Pentecostal ones, turn their own performance into the only relevant context and thus cause a convergence of the alien and the familiar, the intelligible and the unintelligible, the ancestral and the hypermodern, as if they were homogeneous components of the same religious artifact. As David Lehmann says, speaking of the Universal Church of the Kingdom of God of Brazil, a prosperous religious multinational, "it adopts imprecations, gestures and symbols drawn directly from the possession cults [of *Camdomblé* and *Umbanda*, Afro-Brazilian religions], but without the slightest hint of a theory of identity or autochtony. It simply borrows them because the leadership or the preachers believe they will work" (1998).

In African contexts, an important feature of these churches is the emphasis on faith healing. While some churches claim to heal all diseases without exception, others make a claim to a particular set of diseases, including economic and financial failures that are interpreted as forms of "barrenness" (Essien, 2004). Many of these cures are broadcast and, indeed, the mass media are playing a vital role in extending the reach of faith. These amplifying mechanisms, through which religious actors radically expand the scale, speed, and directness of their address, become integral to the way that revelation stages itself (Comaroff, 2009: 21). In this context, the performative nature of the gospel becomes central.

These examples illustrate that one is not facing movements that reject participation in economic and political structures in the name of some purely theocratic nostalgia; rather, these are strategies of involvement in said structures, by resorting to their own mechanisms and with the aim of influencing their agenda. This has been quite obvious for decades in the influence exerted by the New Right in American politics and law and is now more and more prevalent in Brazil and other countries. George W. Bush was elected with the overwhelming support of these sectors (and also with the support of traditionalist Catholics, a topic to which I will return). For his term of 2000–2004, "Evangelical Protestants were President Bush's strongest backers giving him nearly nine in ten of their ballots" (Green, 2009: 320).[16] Davidson and Harris (2006) do not hesitate to consider theocratic Christians in the United States a "new form of fascism" insofar as they call for the death penalty for pro-choice advocates, homosexuals, and women who do not abide by traditional gender roles; they also support the legitimacy of keeping non-Christians incarcerated during the recent U.S. wars, argue for allowing children to leave public schools for domestic homeschooling, and hold the Bible up as a truth standard for science. Moreover, they consider the Enlightenment to be anti-Christian, along with the liberal democracy derived from the Enlightenment and the French Revolution.

Traces of the same conservative politics are also visible in Europe. For example, in the UK, over the last decade, the British National Party (BNP) has been stressing the "Christian roots" of Europe. Vociferous against Islam, which the BNP sees as a major threat, this party has been strong in demanding economic protectionism and "re-nationalization" of the UK, an approach that was successful enough to elect two members to the European parliament in 2009. However, the strong emphasis on the ethnic conception of nationalism that defines British identity (by race and ancestry), at the core of the political campaign of BNP, was not successful in the 2014 elections for the European parliament. The strong anti-Islamic mobilization of BNP failed to reelect any candidate, as many voters "who shared their alienation and opposition to immigration would nonetheless refuse to back a party they saw as compromising democratic principles."[17]

Religious fundamentalisms and women

As in Islamic fundamentalism, the issue of women's rights is a relevant criterion for identifying Christian fundamentalism.[18] As the multiple cases discussed in this book show, religious fundamentalism is not monolithic. Indeed, based on it, the most divergent political projects have been propounded. However, the diverse fundamentalisms and fundamentalist movements present in the contemporary world display a number of similarities, most notably concerning the interpretation of the family, gender roles, and interpersonal relations. According to Hoda Rouhana, the ideologies behind religious fundamentalisms show little respect for the principles of human rights and have little tolerance for people of other faiths. This is particularly striking concerning women—their status, rights, roles, and responsibilities (2005: 4). This situation is present in various regions of the world, as Nira Yuval-Davis (1999, 2004), Sylvia Tamale (2009), or Elizabeth Aguiling-Pangalangan (2010) explain. Gita Sahgal and Nira Yuval-Davis argue that "to conform to the strict confines of womanhood within the fundamentalist religious code is a precondition for maintaining and reproducing the fundamentalist version of society" (1992: 7).[19]

According to Casanova, in the Catholic Church the *aggiornamento* of the Second Vatican Concilium brought about important changes, including on women issues: "an official, relatively uniform, and swift reform from above that found little contestation from below and could easily be enforced across the Catholic world, generating as a result a remarkable global homogenization of Catholic culture at least among the elites" (2005: 101). Nevertheless, large sectors of the Catholic Church *magisterium* would go on subscribing to male chauvinistic ideas very similar to those expounded by the already quoted mentor of the American New Right, Jerry Falwell. As he says, "God Almighty created men and women biologically different and with differing needs and roles. He made men and women to complement each other and to love each other" (1980: 136). The Catholic Church did not hesitate, either, to associate itself with the most reactionary governments of Islamic countries in order to try to counter the formulations of the Beijing Platform concerning the reproductive rights of women.[20]

Similar alliances have taken place recurrently in different contexts. According to Nira Yuval-Davis, the combined rise of Jewish and Christian fundamentalisms in the USA, in alliance with conservative republican politics, has produced a destructive impact on women's rights (2004: 30–32). The persistent invocation of the woman's primordial role as mother and wife, where involvement in matters outside the family is pursued only if it does not interfere with these main duties, accentuates the perpetuation of gender stereotyping and often other forms of discrimination and exclusion as well. This explains why, throughout the world, antifundamentalist women are at the forefront of struggles not just for sexual equality but also for a just peace, antiracism, and human rights—all anathema to national, ethnic, and religious fundamentalists. Women's struggles in various African countries illustrate the magnitude of the challenges ahead. In Uganda and Mozambique, for example, women activists for family law reform (Tamale, 2009; Arthur et al., 2011) have joined forces with Muslim antifundamentalist groups. In both contexts the social movements are confronting narrow definitions of "family" and conservative calls to preserve "the family" as ways of obstructing the recognition of women's rights. While in Mozambique an organized civil society promoted by women's groups won a huge battle to prevent some serious antiwomen laws from being included in the country's new penal code,[21] in Uganda the situation is very different.

Chapter 5

Human Rights in the Contact Zones with Political Theologies

IN LIGHT OF THE DISCUSSIONS in the preceding chapters, it becomes clear that the challenges posed by political theologies to human rights and the ways they relate to contradictory processes of globalization require a more specific and differentiating analysis. That is what I propose to do in this and the next chapters.

The rise of political theologies generates new contact zones among rival conceptions of human dignity, social ordering, and social transformation, with new forms of political, cultural, and ideological turbulence deriving therefrom, which in turn impact human rights in a very particular way. In general, contact zones are social fields in which different cultural lifeworlds meet, mediate, negotiate, and clash. Contact zones are, therefore, zones in which rival normative ideas, knowledges, power forms, symbolic universes, and agencies meet in usually unequal conditions and resist, reject, assimilate, imitate, translate, and subvert each other, thus giving rise to hybrid cultural constellations in which the inequality of exchanges may be either reinforced or reduced. Complexity is intrinsic to the definition of the contact zone itself. Who gets to define who or what belongs to the contact zone and who and what does not? How to define the line that delimits the contact zone? Is the difference between cultures or normative lifeworlds so wide as to make them incommensurable? How to approximate the cultural and normative universes so as to bring them "within visual contact," so to speak? Mary Louise Pratt defines contact zones as "social spaces where disparate cultures meet, clash and grapple with each other often in highly asymmetrical relations of domination and subordination—like colonialism, slavery or their aftermaths as they are lived out across the globe today" (1992: 4). In this formulation, contact zones seem to involve encounters among cultural totalities. This is not necessarily the case. The contact zone may involve selected and partial cultural differences, those that in a given time-space find themselves in competition to provide meaning for a given course of action. Moreover, the unequal exchanges extend today far beyond colonialism and its aftermath even though, as postcolonial studies have shown, colonialism continues to play a much more important role today than one may be ready to admit.

The political, cultural, and ideological turbulence deriving from the rise of political theologies brings new light to the limits of human rights politics on a global scale. In this chapter, I point out the following dimensions and manifestations of this turbulence: the turbulence among rival principles; the turbulence between roots and options; and the turbulence between the sacred and the profane, the religious and the secular, the transcendent and the immanent.

Turbulence among rival principles

The turbulence among rival principles must be analyzed in the context of an old tension that inhabits human rights and results from the discrepancy between principles and practices, a discrepancy that is indeed much older than human rights. It is present in most cultures and social systems, but is particularly salient in societies inspired by Christianity. In the thirteenth century, Thomas Aquinas (1948) identified it perfectly when he criticized the Christians of his time for what he called *habitus principiorum*: the habit of obsessively invoking Christian principles to allow themselves to fail to observe them in practice. Western modernity inherited this *habitus* and turned it into a principle of political action, consecrated by modern constitutionalism: The catalogues of human rights recognized by modern constitutions became increasingly inclusive, but the prevailing political practices went on committing or tolerating violations, often mass violations, of human rights. This inconsistency today has reached unprecedented levels, particularly since neoliberal globalization has grounded the legitimacy of social change on three principles, all of them extremely vulnerable to the discrepancy between principles and practices: democracy, human rights, and the rule of law.

Progressive theologies have played an important role in reinforcing nonconformism before the hypocrisy of conventional human rights thinking and practice. Indeed, one of the most vivid manifestations of the social and economic cleavage between the Global North and the Global South is the discrepancy between supposedly emancipatory principles and the practices that, in the name of such principles, contribute to reproducing oppression and injustice—

when they don't bring about the destruction of entire countries, as illustrated recently with utmost cruelty in the Middle East. Whenever human rights are part of counterhegemonic struggles—whether for canceling the debt of poor countries, for access to land and water, or for self-determination of indigenous peoples—they undergo a process of political and philosophical reconstruction that renders all the more visible and condemnable the discrepancy between principles and practices that underlies the hegemonic liberal, imperialist human rights complex.

The resilience of the discrepancy between principles and practices and the hypocrisy of conventional human rights in this regard have fueled the current turbulence among rival principles in the contact zone. The historical failure of "universal" human rights in bringing about ways of collective and individual life that are consonant with their principles has opened the space for the cultural and political reemergence of alternative principles. Human rights principles are therefore confronted with other grammars of human dignity, be they those underlying political theologies, or those embedded in the lifeworlds of indigenous peoples and their ancestral, non-Western cosmovisions. The cleavage between rival principles is especially visible in the conflict between Western-based globalization, whether hegemonic or counterhegemonic, and the rise of non-Christian political theologies. This cleavage adds new dimensions to the question of global social justice as the issue of socioeconomic injustice is compounded with the issue of cognitive injustice, that is, the historical record of unequal relations among different kinds of knowledge and worldviews. Coming after a long succession of formulas—the "civilizing mission," progress, development, and modernization—neoliberal globalization pursues a global imperial project, based on clearly Western and Christian principles finely consistent with conventional human rights: a separation between immanence and transcendence and a specular conception of the relation between them; individual autonomy in economy and politics (common interest based on the pursuit of self-interest); secularization (the separation of church and state, and the transference of divine omnipotence to the secular state); the separation of nature and society, the former being conceived of as the latter's ever available resource; progress as a secular version of redemption; and a distinction between public and private space, religion belonging to the latter.

These conceptions have always clashed with other rival conceptions. The peoples that entered the zone of contact with Western modernity did so under conditions of enforced inferiority, as was typically the case with colonialism.

Many were forced to abandon the conceptions that had guided them before they reached (or were violently thrown into) the contact zone; others adopted the new conceptions more or less willingly or appropriated them by changing their meanings. The strength of the new conceptions conveyed by Western modernity seldom resided in the conceptions themselves but rather in the power of those wanting to impose them. Throughout a multisecular history there were alternating periods of more or less violent imposition (between war and conversion, pillage and trade, assimilationism and multiculturalism).

The imposition of monocultural logics took many forms.[1] They produced a wide range of populations and ways of being, living, and knowing that were considered ignorant, inferior, particular, residual, or unproductive, whatever the case might be. Such classifications were established in an authoritarian way, always at the service of a project of economic, political, social, and cultural domination. Among all the non-Western peoples (cultures and sociabilities) that were subjected to this colonial and imperial project, Islamic peoples have probably more than any others clearly identified their submission to such a project as a historical defeat. The memory of periods of great cultural, political, and social flourishing and even hegemony in large parts of the world has no doubt a lot to do with this. The defeat and the memory of it passed on from generation to generation must have contributed decisively to making Islamic peoples feel their historical options in an especially radical and dilemmatic way. Either they could imitate Western modernity, its principles and monocultures, and thereby lose their identity, deny their glorious past, and become strangers to themselves (imitation, alienation, strangeness), or they could radically reject modernity and accept the costs of continuing to live in a time patterned centuries ago by hostile principles and monocultures, which not only dominated but humiliated them as well (rejection and alternative social project). The first option seems to have prevailed in the period of Arab nationalism mentioned earlier (and which in fact spread far beyond the Arab world), when the slogan was "modernizing Islam." The second option, in turn, seems to prevail today in political Islam, the slogan being "Islamizing modernity," or, in the case of fundamentalist theologies, to reject modernity altogether. In the contact zone of human rights and Islamic theologies, this option contributes the most today to create turbulence among rival principles.[2]

The turbulence among rival principles derives from politically organized nonconformism vis-à-vis the historical defeat of a given set of principles—be it the defeat of the medieval church (with its Christendom project) or the defeat of Islam by Western imperialism—along with the refusal to accept it as irreversible. The issue is not to measure distances, since the rival principles are often viewed as incommensurable and all of them claim to be ultimate. In a way, we are facing rival monocultures. In these conditions, the contact zone tends to assume a particularly confrontational character, and the negotiations and compositions can be imagined only on the basis of laborious procedures of intercultural mediation and translation.[3]

The turbulence between roots and options

The second dimension of turbulence in the contact zone having an impact on human rights is the turbulence between roots and options.[4] This kind of turbulence traverses all the contact zones between human rights and political theologies, a turbulence that affects the cleavage both between the Global North and the Global South, and between the Global West and the Global non-West. This particular turbulence raises a third issue of justice at the heart of the contact zone: historical, postcolonial justice. What follows applies in general to changes in the binary roots/options brought about by political theologies, particularly by the fundamentalist ones. The social construction of identity and change in Western modernity is based on an equation of roots and options. Such an equation confers a dual character on modern thought: on the one hand, it is a thought of roots, on the other, a thought of options. The thought of roots concerns all that is profound, permanent, singular, and unique, all that provides reassurance and consistency; the thought of options concerns all that is variable, ephemeral, replaceable, and indeterminate from the viewpoint of roots. The major difference between roots and options is scale. Roots are large-scale entities. As in cartography, they cover vast symbolic territories and long historical durations, but fail to map the characteristics of the field in detail and without ambiguity. Theirs is, therefore, a map that guides as much as it misguides. In contrast, options are small-scale entities. They cover confined territories and short durations, but do so in enough detail to allow for the assessment of the risk involved in the choice of alternative options. Because of this difference of scale, roots are unique, while options are multiple. The root/option duality is a founding duality; that is to say, it is not subjected to the play it itself institutes between roots and options. In other words, one does not have the option not to think in terms of roots and options.

The efficacy of the equation lies in a double cunning. First, there is the cunning of the equilibrium between the past and the future. The thought of roots presents itself as a thought of the past as opposed to the thought of the future, which the thought of options alone is supposed to be. I speak of cunning because, in fact, both are thoughts of the future. In this equation, the past remains largely underrepresented, which is not the same as oblivion. On the contrary, the past may manifest itself as "excessive memory," to use Charles Maier's expression (1993: 137). There is underrepresentation whenever memory becomes an exercise in melancholy, which, rather than recovering the past, neutralizes its redemptive potential by substituting evocation for the struggle against failing expectations.

The second kind of cunning concerns the equilibrium between roots and options. This equation presents itself as symmetry: an equilibrium of roots and options, and in the distribution of options. Indeed, it is not so. On the one hand, options are overwhelmingly predominant. Although certain social groups or historical moments consider roots predominant and others consider options to be so, it is in fact always a question of options. While certain kinds of options imply the discursive primacy of roots, others imply their marginalization. The equilibrium is impossible. Depending on the historical moment or social group, either roots precede options or options precede roots. The play is always from roots to options and from options to roots; the only variable is the power of each term as a narrative of identity and change. On the other hand, there is no equilibrium or equity in the social distribution of options. Quite the opposite occurs: Roots are but constellations of determinations that, as they define the field of options, also define the social groups that have access to it and those that do not.

A few examples will help illustrate this historical process. To begin with, it is in the light of this equation of roots and options that modern Western society sees medieval society and distinguishes itself from it. European medieval society is seen as one in which the primacy of roots is total, whether as regards religion, theology, or tradition. This medieval society is not necessarily a static society, but it evolves according to a logic of roots. On the contrary, modern society sees itself as a dynamic society that evolves according to a logic of options. This it proves by assuming as founding root the social contract and the general will sustaining it. The social contract is the founding metaphor of a radical option—the option to leave the state of nature and to inaugurate civil society—which turns into a root that makes everything possible, except to return to the state of nature. The contractuality of roots is irreversible, such being the limit of the reversibility of options. The paramountcy in Western modernity of concepts such as individualism, citizenship, human rights, civil society, markets, the civic nation, and constitutional patriotism signals the priority given to the logic of options, which, in any case, and as we just saw, are options based on roots. This self-description of Western modernity led it to conceive of not just medieval society but all other cultures and societies as based on roots and, accordingly, on the paramountcy of primordialism, status, identity, community, ethnicity, and the ethnic nation, disregarding the fact that in all societies the logic of roots operates in conjunction with a logic of options.

Whatever their previous experiences, the cultures that entered the contact zone with Western modernity were forced to define themselves in terms of the equation between roots and options. They did so both to resist and to adapt themselves to the modern equation. While defining the terms of the conflict, Western modernity engaged in a brutal redistribution of the past, present, and future of the peoples and cultures in the contact zone. It reserved the future for itself and allowed various pasts to coexist with it, as long as they all converged into the same future: its own. That is to say, it ascribed to the dominated peoples and cultures neutralized pasts that lacked the capacity to produce alternative futures vis-à-vis Western modernity. The various independences did not mean a break with this macro theory of history; to a large extent they furthered it, and this is why the contact zone continued to be a colonial zone, in spite of the end of political colonialism.

Surprising affinities between neoliberal globalization and fundamentalist theologies

The high turbulence that now affects the equation between roots and options is bound to have a broad impact on all social and cultural experiences and trajectories that meet or confront each other in the contact zone, even though such an impact will reflect the asymmetries that ground the contact zone. On the side of hegemonic Western modernity, the intensification of neoliberal globalization radicalizes options through the loss of roots. The social contract, conceived of as roots to start with, is being transformed into one option among many others: the neoliberal movement away from the social contract and toward possessive individual contractualism. Thus, the foundational move from the state of nature to civil society inscribed in liberal political theory, at first thought to be irreversible, reveals itself to be reversible after all. The increasingly larger social groups that are banned from the social contract (postcontractualism) or do not even have access to it (precontractualism) become discardable populations. Without minimal citizenship rights, they are indeed cast into a new state of nature, what I call social fascism (Santos, 2002b: 453–57). In such conditions, options may multiply themselves indefinitely, since they are freed from the constraints of roots. In reality—the reality of unemployed and low-paid workers, immigrants, indebted families and students, the impoverished middle classes—the greater the abstract autonomy to select among options, the smaller the concrete capacity of doing so.

On the part of the cultures and societies that were historically colonized by Western modern capitalism, particularly as regards Islamic cultures and societies, an apparently opposite process is occurring: the radicalization of roots (especially strong in the case of the various fundamentalisms), the search for an originary identity, and a glorious past empowering enough to ground an alternative future. In this case, options cease to have any meaning, to the extent that the only alternative consists in resorting to what has no alternative at all: the foundational root. The radicalism of this option is justified by the idea that something went profoundly wrong in history in that such a glorious past was unable to prevent the abysmal humiliation of the present and the total blockage of the future.

Notwithstanding the many differences between the processes of turbulence in the equation between roots and options in Western societies and in Islamic societies, intriguing similarities can be observed. For instance, Christian fundamentalisms and Islamic fundamentalisms share the same abysmal fear of the future, however expressed in different forms. Fundamentalist Islam exorcises the future through its radical and politicized recourse to the past, thereby converting it into an all-empowering past, an all-supporting non-Western root that does not allow for options. It invests in a kind of future that can only be conceived of as the future's past. The same is true of the various versions of Christian fundamentalist theologies. However, in their case, because of their Western identity, it is not possible to imagine a non-Western past uncontaminated by the factors that led to the current predicament. Their fear of the future is transmuted into an uncompromising (in extreme cases, even suicidal) uneasiness before the intolerable repetition of the present. As Walter Benjamin (1977) has shown so well, having neutralized the past a long time ago, the West, unable to resort to the past, resorts to the radical repetition of the present (the end of history), which is another way of expressing a fear of the future.

A second similarity resides in the polarization between authoritarian processes of depoliticization and repoliticization, leading to the extreme instrumentalization of matters of principle. The latter is clearly observable in fundamentalist Islamic theologies. The politicization of the past implies the instrumentalization of attributes deemed to be matters of principle and therefore unavailable, namely the *shari'a*. The modern state is either to be destroyed or to be occupied and managed according to the logic of religious rulership. The principle of the sovereignty of the people is unacceptable in light of the transcendent all-governing will of God as it is transmitted to religious leaders. The latter can only be accountable before God, not before any democratic forum. The interpretation given to the sacred texts has absolute value because, rather than interpretation, it is in fact revealed truth. Regarding neoliberal globalization, celebrated in general with enthusiasm by most Christian fundamentalisms, the erosion of the social contract as a root renders possible the instrumental use of all the principles derived from it, namely the rule of law, democracy, and human rights. The symptoms of such instrumentalization are multiple: extreme levels of social inequality in light of which the formal equality before the law becomes a cruel joke; an extreme power concentration that hollows out the democratic process and manipulates democratic representation and participation beyond recognition; price tags on every social value through which a socially useful market economy slides into a morally repugnant market society; the erosion of social and economic rights and the rise of an uncivil society and/or of the social fascism that goes with it; appalling double standards in evaluating human rights performances; and using the war on terrorism as a pretext to control citizens, promulgate secret laws to be adjudicated by secret courts, criminalize social protest, and erode civil and political rights to such a point that citizenship becomes undistinguishable from subjection. Given the radical instrumentalization to which human rights are thus being subjected, they become foreign inside Western modernity itself. It is more and more obvious and disturbing that the superiority of Western modernity sustains itself only on the basis of the negation of everything that it has offered historically as a justification of its superiority. The instrumentalization of the rule of law and human rights is particularly patent in the case of Christian fundamentalist and integrist theologies, in which the legitimacy structuring societies resides in God's law and not in human laws. The utter unavailability of law as a root becomes a disguise for its free instrumentalization as an option. Although Joseph Ratzinger's theology does not show many of the features of a fundamentalist theology (such as the inerrancy of the Bible and its consequent literalist interpretation), his political thinking reveals fundamentalist streaks. Consider, for example, two of his statements on freedom and on the legitimacy of the state. On freedom, derived from modernity: "Fundamentally, in the modern age, behind the radical desire for freedom, there is the promise: you will be like God. . . . The implicit aim of all modern freedom movements is, after all, to be like a god, to depend on nothing or nobody, not to be limited in one's freedom by another's freedom. . . . The Jacobine version of the idea of liberation (let's thus call modern radicalisms) is a rebellion against the being of man, a rebellion against the truth, and, therefore—as Sartre saw so insightfully—it leads man to an existence of contradiction to which we call hell" (1993: 219–20). As regards the state: "A State that on principle wants itself agnostic vis-à-vis religion and God, and grounds the Law solely on the opinion of the majority, tends to reduce itself to the level of an association of wrongdoers. Here, we must commend the decisive interpretation of Platonic tradition proposed by Augustine: when God is excluded, the organization law of wrongdoers emerges, whether shamelessly or mitigated" (1993: 90).

Both in the current hegemonic version of Western modernity, neoliberal globalization, and in fundamentalist political theologies, authoritarianism feeds on the reduction of the public space and the crisis of the state, and reinforces both of them. Resignation rather than politically negotiated consensus, conversion rather than conversation becomes a priority. Again, in spite of the many differences separating them, neoliberal globalization and Islamic and Christian fundamentalist theologies alike are revealing destructive dynamics that manifest themselves through new extremisms. Their names are, among others: war, market, jihad, terrorism, the war on terror, state terrorism, antiterrorism laws, martyrs, suicide bombers, heroes, enemy combatants, restrictive immigration laws, disposable or discardable populations, the Patriot Act, Guantánamo, unilateralism, preemptive war, and national security instead of human security.[5] But the most disturbing form of extremism is what I designate as sacrificial violence. Sacrificial violence is the immolation of what is most precious allegedly in order to save it. In the case of Islamic fundamentalism, sacrificial violence is carried out against what is considered to be the intolerable oppression and humiliation by Western capitalist and imperial interests. In the case of the most aggressive forms of neoliberal globalization (imperialism and neocolonialism), life is destroyed to "save" life; human rights are violated to "defend" human rights; the conditions for democracy are destroyed to "promote" democracy.[6] The Middle East is currently the privileged ground for the exercise of sacrificial violence by neoliberal capitalism. The two forms of sacrificial violence, Islamic and Western, however similar, are not symmetrical. According to each one's relevant community, both are justified as defensive. But if the extreme imbalances of destructive power are taken into account, it is difficult not to see Islamic sacrificial violence as defensive and Western-based sacrificial violence as aggressive.

The turbulence to which the equation between roots and options in the contact zone is subjected shows that the drama of fundamentalist political Islam is also the drama of hegemonic Western modernity under the form of neoliberal globalization, notwithstanding their glaring differences, the most glaring being the fact that modernity has on its side the brute force of global capitalism and military superiority. What is tragic above all is that the dynamics proper to each of these dramas prevents them from acknowledging their own disturbing similarities. In point of fact, only a profound social, political, and cultural redistribution of the past and future would reveal that the two dramas are looking at each other in the same mirror. Such redistribution would entail the fulfillment of historical and postcolonial justice, the third dimension of justice, alongside socioeconomic and cognitive justice.

The turbulence between the sacred and the profane, the religious and the secular, the transcendent and the immanent

This turbulence shows, more dramatically than any other, the cleavages between human rights and Western modernity, on one side, and political theologies and, in particular, fundamentalist political theologies, on the other. In this regard, what is most evident at the outset is the number of radical differences among the conceptions that confront each other in the contact zone. Fundamentalist or integrist political theologies understand turbulence, in this regard, as resulting from the fact that as yet not all the profane has been reduced to the sacred, the secular to the religious, the immanent to the transcendent. The consensual understanding of religion in Islam, that it should be omnipresent and permeate all dimensions of life equally, is converted by fundamentalist political Islam into the ultimate political rule. In other words, religion is converted into a political weapon wielded against all vestiges of secularization left over from the projects to modernize Arab nationalism, which are deemed to have failed.[7] Hence the frontal attack on the secular state, on the separation of public and private spaces, and on all the institutions that claim to be governed by rules foreign to the *shari'a*. Fundamentalist political Islam is a geopolitical project that asserts itself as a theocracy. Its universalization occurs by means of the universalization of the religion of Islam. Given its territorial confinement, the state cannot serve the project of universalizing Islam, unless it is governed by religious leaders, whose *magisterium* and power are extraterritorial. The resurgence of this type of Islamic political theology was made visible by the 1979 Iranian revolution and has consolidated itself in the last three decades.[8]

The contrast of this stance with the political assumptions underlying human rights and Western modernity could not be greater. For the latter, religion was early on transferred from the public to the private space, a historical process known as secularization. Its foundational moment may be dated from 1648, the date of the Treaty of Westphalia, which put an end to the religious wars known as the Thirty Years' War. The separation between the spiritual power of the church and the temporal power of the modern state was a very complex historical process that assumed different forms in different countries, regions of the world, and historical periods. It did not prevent religion, for example, from being put at the service of colonialism as an integral part of the civilizing mission. By the same token, if it is true that, according to the Enlightenment, religion would became an anachronism—its being consigned to the private space was considered a transitional phase toward its total disappearance—it is no less true that the power of the state constituted itself through a complex play of mirrors with the sacred power of the church, assuming many of the latter's sacred and ritual characteristics (Marramao, 1994: 23). Not to mention the "Christian values" that, through the theories of natural law from the seventeenth century onward, had a great impact on the conception of human rights. Moreover, and at a deeper level, seen from the "outside," from a non-Christian, non-Western perspective, secularism (which should be distinguished from secularity)[9] is as much a part of Christianity as Christian religion. Secularism and Christian religion were part of the same colonial "package."[10] They were also close partners in the imposition of a monoculture of Western scientific knowledge through which so much epistemicide (the suppression of peasant, indigenous, and other rival non-Western knowledges) has been committed (Santos, 2004; 2007a; 2014).

One of the paradoxes of this conception is the fact that Christian influence coexists with the right to freedom of religion. Carl Schmitt even argues in his *Political Theology* (1922) that all the concepts pertaining to the power of the state are secularized versions of theological concepts.[11] This viewpoint, focused on the limits of secularization in Western societies, is being widely discussed once again due in part to the challenges posed by Islam and, especially, political

Islam. In the words of Teresa Toldy, "Western societies seem to have awakened from the 'secularist dream'" (2011: 3).[12]

Be that as it may, claiming the autonomy of the power of the state vis-à-vis religion is one of the fundamental attributes of the separation between public and private space in Western modernity. Perhaps for this very reason, however, the fate of religion in Western modernity is closely linked to the distinction between public and private space. The stabilization of religion was the correlate of the stabilization, by means of religion, of the oppressions and fears of the private space, as feminist theologies and sociologies have forcefully shown. It so happens that this space has never been stabilized itself, if for no other reason than because it is intimately linked to transformations occurring in the public space.[13] The amplitude of the public sphere, conceived of as the domain of the political, has always been conditioned by the intensity of democracy and the public policies (especially the social policies) of the democratic state. By enlarging the social fields of nonmarket relations (in education, health, and social welfare), the state developed strategies of legitimation and trust that met with the loyalty of the citizens toward the state (Santos, 2002b). At the same time, such strategies allowed for the institutionalization of the social conflicts and the public debates they stirred.

For the past thirty years and from different and even opposing political perspectives, the modern distinction between the public and the private sphere has been questioned. On the one hand, it has been questioned by social movements, particularly by feminist and gay and lesbian movements for which, against the liberal understanding, the private space is political as well and therefore has to be the object of public debate and political decisions. Only in this way will it be possible to put an end to the oppressions and discriminations reproduced inside the private space. Thus, the private space stopped being the limit of the political and became one of the fields of the political. Paradoxically, this expansion of the private sphere occurred in tandem with the contraction of the public sphere. Various factors contributed to the shrinking of the public space: the crisis of the national state, provoked or deepened by hegemonic globalization; the erosion of social policies; the deinstitutionalization of the relations between labor and capital; the increase of authoritarianism on the part of state and nonstate actors; the mediatization of politics and the personalization of political power; and the privatization of public services. As a result, the doubly binding relation between the public and the private spheres becomes apparent. As the public sphere shrinks and more and more dimensions of collective life become depoliticized, the private space—thereby turned into the foundation of the political autonomy of the individual—expands symbolically and materially. Religion emerges then as one of the central features of such an expansion. With the weakening of the safety nets created by the welfare state, the individual becomes vulnerable to fear, insecurity, and the loss of hope. As Feuerbach and Marx showed in the mid-1800s, religion has always fed on this vulnerability (Feuerbach, [1841] 1957; Marx, [1843] 1964). It may also be argued that the retreat of the secularized transcendence of the state invites the need for an alternative transcendence, one that indeed has always been there.

These social and political conditions have been the breeding ground for conservative political theologies and their radical attacks on the public/private distinction, particularly in the case of the fundamentalist theologies for which sacred time and space has an absolute command over profane time and space. This resurgence of conservative, traditionalist political theologies has been quite visible since the mid-1970s in the three Abrahamic religions: Judaism, Christianity, and Islam. To the extent that they put an end to civic and democratic debate in their areas of intervention, traditionalist theologies in general shrink the public space. Capitalizing on the crisis of the legitimacy of the state and the consequent crisis of republican values, traditionalist theologies are both the cause and the consequence of the crisis of the historical project of secularization.[14]

Are other human rights possible?

The preceding analysis shows the magnitude of the clashes that are occurring in the contact zone. Actually, it is rather a wide set of contact zones, and the asymmetries of power in the contact zones are obvious. Such asymmetries derive in great measure from the imperial, neocolonial nature of contemporary world (dis)order. The oldest asymmetries are almost a thousand years old, if we date them from the Crusades; or more than five centuries, if we date them from the European expansion. What is new about them is, on the one hand, the range and intensity of the fluxes in the contact zone and, on the other hand, the new forms of fear and resistance. These new features are responsible for the discursive and practical fragility of human rights in contact zones. The stronger the questions raised, the more clearly apparent is the weakness of the answer given by human rights.

This does not mean that human rights must be discarded. On the contrary, it has never been so important not to squander ideas and practices that at least potentially may sustain resistance against oppression, domination, and discrimination. It means that only by recognizing the current fragilities of human rights is it possible to construct, out of them, but also beyond them, strong ideas and practices of resistance. Such reconstruction will enable human rights to become an instrument of struggle and resistance as well as an alternative, no matter how limited. The complexity of interactions, conflicts, and commitments in the contact zone manifests itself in the three turbulences I have identified, which are the result of three disjunctions or discrepancies: between rival principles, between roots and options, and between the religious and the secular. These disjunctions intersect with unequal relations of economic, social, political, and cultural power, and the turbulences derive from the intensification of the conflicts they stir. Seen from an ethical and political perspective, the different turbulences reflect different dimensions of the global injustice constitutive of the imperial order in its most recent phase, neoliberal globalization as the new guise of monopoly capitalism: socioeconomic injustice, cognitive injustice (including epistemological, sexual, racial, and religious injustice), and historical injustice. This means that the different forms of global social injustice have no separate existence and that, therefore, each of them is present in all the others. Even so, it is important and possible to distinguish them in order to identify the different kinds of conflicts and the various actors and resistances.

The turbulence among rival principles reveals both socioeconomic and cognitive injustice.[15] Socioeconomic injustice derives from unfulfilled promises and from the many inequalities and discriminations that are not considered human rights violations or are silenced by the dominant discourses and practices of human rights. Cognitive injustice derives from the confrontational actions and interpretations between distinct cultural paradigms, ethical principles, and forms of rationality. Global cognitive justice claims a new relationalism capable of creating a vernacular cosmopolitanism from the bottom up,[16] that is, a new relationalism between races, sexes, kinds of knowledge, and ways of being. The fragility of human rights, as far as global cognitive injustice is concerned, derives from the fact that the dominant conceptions and practices of human rights themselves produce cognitive injustice. They do so, not because their assumptions are Western, but because of the unilateral way in which, on their basis, they construct abstract universal claims. Here, the solution is not relativism, but rather a new relationalism.

The turbulence between roots and options raises a third dimension of social injustice, namely historical injustice. Historical injustice is closely related to cognitive injustice, but it may be distinguished from it because it focuses on the theories and practices of history that have produced an unfair distribution of the possibilities and potentialities provided by each historical time. To redress historical injustice means, therefore, reparation, alternatives to capitalist development, and the decolonization of interstates, as well as interpeoples and interpersonal relations. As a result of historical injustice, many peoples, cultures, and sociabilities were ascribed or had a past imposed upon them—a past without a future—by other peoples, cultures, and sociabilities, which thereby claimed for themselves a future unencumbered by the past. The former were forced to forget their past and the future in order to live the present; the latter turned the present into the instant ratification of the past and the fleeting moment at which the pathos of future social change is ignited.

This historical injustice can only be revealed in the light of a postcolonial, historical theory and practice. And herein lies the specific fragility of the answer of human rights in this domain. Conventional human rights thinking and practice conceives human rights as ahistorical. Hence, as I mentioned in chapter 1, the difficulty in recognizing the collective rights of peoples and social groups that were victims of historical oppressions and the impossibility of seeing in the violations of human rights, acknowledged as such, the symptom of other and much more serious violations.[17] Hence, finally, the impossibility of seeing in the unequal relations between the Global North and the Global South, the Global West and the Global non-West, unfathomable violations of human rights.

Lastly, the turbulence concerning the relations between the sacred and the profane, the transcendent and the immanent, the religious and the secular is a turbulence in which the collision between conventional human rights and political theologies appears most fully. The weakness of the answer of human rights in this domain derives from three factors. On the one hand, human rights assume their secularization as a fait accompli, rather than as a historical process that is full of contradictions. On the other hand, human rights ignore their own unfinished and contradictory character as they favor secularization without questioning the Christian and Western conceptions of human dignity underlying them. Finally, by reducing the issue of religion to religious freedom, human rights turn religion into a private resource, an object of consumption disengaged from its relations of production. They cannot, therefore, distinguish between the religion of the oppressors and the religion of the oppressed.

In light of the challenges posed by political theologies, the reinvention of human rights and their transformation as an instrument of social emancipation in different cultural contexts demands an exercise in intercultural translation

(Santos, 2004; 2006b: 131–47; 2014) and diatopical hermeneutics (Panikkar, 1979; Santos, 1995: 273–78; 2007c: 23–26; 2014) through which the reciprocal limitations of alternative conceptions of human dignity can be identified, thus opening the possibility of new relations and dialogues among them. This is what I call the *ecology of knowledges* (Santos, 2006a: 401–36; 2007a: 3–40; 2014), an epistemological exercise based on the incompleteness of any single body of knowledge and aimed at identifying different knowledges and criteria of rigor and validity that operate credibly in social practices with the view of developing creative interactions among them. The objective of the ecology of knowledges is to broaden the intellectual and cultural legitimacy of the struggles for securing human dignity. The possibility and the success of such an exercise calls for some specification here.

According to traditionalist political theologies, human rights are a secular usurpation of the rights of God. These divine rights, as revealed to the church and church leaders, are the only legitimate source of rights and entail more duties than rights. In the light of such premises, an ecology of knowledges regarding human rights and traditionalist political theologies is not possible.[18] From the point of view of the latter, because they are a human construction, human rights lack the legitimacy necessary to engage in dialogue with a divine construction. On the contrary, I see a great potential for intercultural translation between reconstructed human rights and progressive pluralistic political theologies—whether Christian, Islamic, or others. According to the latter, conventional human rights politics is little else than institutionalized hypocrisy politics. In contrast, other conceptions of human rights—counterhegemonic and intercultural—may contribute to strengthening or enlarging the social struggles anchored in progressive pluralistic theologies. The intercultural enrichment of the conceptions of human dignity not only will strengthen the legitimacy of the struggles conducted in its name, but will also help to privilege the conceptions that most directly confront the dimensions of social injustice I have identified in this book. I do not think that, within the ambit of progressive theologies, this task will be exceedingly difficult. For instance, the fact that Islam does not accept a secularized conception of human dignity,[19] and that Christian theologies think that human dignity is rooted in the image and semblance of God,[20] is not an obstacle to finding in their sacred books and law (both *shari'a* and the Bible) conceptions of human dignity that are not incommensurate in practice with the conception of human dignity underlying human rights.

The rise of political theologies has at least had the historical merit of putting in a new light the limitations, peculiarities, and fragilities of conventional human rights politics. The work of reconstruction or even reinvention of human rights cannot but be enormous, if human rights are to face all the dimensions of global injustice analyzed in this book and provide credible answers to the strong questions raised by global injustice. Such a work of reconstruction and reinvention of human rights is neither a utopia nor too remote an objective. It is actually happening right now and assuming surprising forms. For example, until recently it would be unthinkable to imagine the constitution of a country adopting a new relation between human nature and non-human nature, extending to nature the philosophy of human rights, thus guaranteeing the rights of nature. Yet this is precisely what is established by Article 71 of the Constitution of Ecuador, approved by national referendum in 2008. Article 71 states: "Nature, or Pacha Mama, has the right to have its existence fully respected, together with the maintenance and regeneration of its vital cycles, structure, and evolutionary processes." In this conception of nature as Mother Earth, the impact of indigenous cosmogony and ontology is clearly reflected.[21]

As I have tried to show, the fragility of hegemonic human rights does not merely lie in the fact that they provide weak answers to the strong questions confronting us in our time. It lies mainly in the fact that hegemonic human rights do not acknowledge the pertinence or seriousness of many of those strong questions. The struggle for a counterhegemonic politics of human rights must start from such an acknowledgement. Once the latter takes place, new possibilities emerge for a mutually enriching exchange between counterhegemonic human rights politics and progressive political theologies. In the next chapter, I will explore some such possibilities.

Chapter 6

Toward a Postsecularist Conception of Human Rights

Counterhegemonic Human Rights and Progressive Theologies

THE KIND OF COUNTERHEGEMONIC HUMAN RIGHTS I have been proposing in this book can only be imagined as a struggle against unjust human suffering, conceived in its broadest sense, and as an effort to encompass nature as an integral part of humanity. The twentieth century was an antihumanist century, and for very good reasons. In many respects, it carried a progressive critique of the abstract Enlightenment humanism that contributed to trivialize and silence the human degradation that occurred under the forms of domination present in capitalist societies, such as patriarchy and colonialism. Another rarely acknowledged source of antihumanism was the so-called "death of God." Once the capacity of human beings to transform reality seemed potentially infinite, Western modernity in essence made God superfluous. In a very personal and dramatic way, Blaise Pascal (1966) realized that without God such a capacity was also potentially destructive. According to Pascal, thinking of God is the highest form of human thought, and depriving human beings of that act is equivalent to depriving them of the highest regard for other human beings. This most pious formulation of the presence of God was fully (and perversely) confirmed centuries later by the most impious formulation of Nietzsche ([1882] 1974): *Gott ist tot* [God is dead]. Nietzsche represents the full accomplishment of the modern project concerning God: from superfluity to utter nonexistence. Contrary to the modern project, however, the death of God in Nietzsche, rather than meaning the final triumph of human beings, represents their final demise, the end of human beings with a capacity to follow moral imperatives or to seek truth, the new possibilities being those of the *Übermensch* [Superman] proclaimed by Zarathustra (Nietzsche, [1883] 2012).

At the beginning of the twenty-first century, religion and theology are back. Yet it is not at all certain that God is back as well, at least, not Pascal's God, as the ultimate guarantor of concrete humanity. On the contrary, the ways in which religions and conservative and fundamentalist theologies proliferate today seem to make God as superfluous as Western modernity's God. God has become the label for a global political enterprise of god-products. But this is not the whole story. Since the 1960s, pluralist, progressive theologies and community-based religious practices have emerged, for which God seems to be revealed in unjust human suffering, in the life experiences of all the victims of domination, oppression, and discrimination. As a consequence, to bear witness to this God means to denounce such suffering and to struggle against it. Both revelation and redemption, or rather, liberation, take place in this world, in the form of a struggle for another world made possible. Herein lies the possibility of connecting the return of God to a transmodern, concrete insurgent humanism.

My argument in this chapter is that a dialogue between human rights and progressive theologies is possible and that it is a good path to develop truly intercultural and more effective emancipatory practices. By mutually enriching themselves, human rights and political theologies may deepen the counterhegemonic potential of both. The result will be an ecology of conceptions of human dignity, some secular some religious, achieved through what I called elsewhere a diatopical hermeneutics (Santos, 1995: 273–78; 2007c: 23–26; 2014), a practice-oriented exercise of transformative interpretation between the *topos* of human rights and the *topoi* of revelation and liberation of progressive political theologies. In the following, I briefly mention some of the ways this might happen.

The human subject both as a concrete individual and as a collective being

Progressive theologies can help to recover the "human" of human rights. Both on the conservative side and on the progressive side, the human has been under siege since the abstractions of the Enlightenment revealed the social and historical vacuity of the concept. From opposite perspectives, the theories of the end of history and the theories of the death of the subject converge to discredit collective and individual resistance against injustice and oppression. The critical skepticism of Theodor Adorno, who declares the death of the individual in consumer society and fails to see an alternative, is particularly telling in this regard. As he says in *Prismen:* "The horror, however, is that the citizen has not found a successor" (1955: 267). Again, the solution propounded by Marxism—the class subject and the "new man" as the agents of history moving forward—is today equally questioned, due to its inability to combine equality and freedom, liberation and autonomy. Progressive theologies have been aware of these dilemmas, while forging historically concrete conceptions of human dignity in which God is the ultimate guarantor of freedom and autonomy in the struggles that subjects, both individual and collective subjects, carry out to become subjects of their own history.

It comes as no surprise that the theologian Johann Baptist Metz, for instance, should draw upon Herbert Marcuse to assert that "solidarity and community do not imply an abandonment of the individual, but are the result of autonomous individual decision and that this solidarity is a solidarity of individuals, not of masses" (Metz, 1980: 69). According to Metz, "the God of the Christian Gospel is, after all, not a God of conquerors, but a God of slaves" (1980: 71). Therefore, to be a subject in God's presence implies being present in the struggle against the kind of oppression and hatred that make it impossible for the mass of the populations in many parts of the world to become subjects. The dialectics of the individual and the collective is well expressed by Metz when he says: "Because of its eschatological proviso over against any abstract concept of progress and humanity, the church protects the individual of the present moment from being used as material and means for the building up of a technological and totally rationalized future. It criticizes the attempt to see individuality merely as a function of a technologically controlled social production" (1968: 13). Similarly, concerning theology, "it has always been very important to political theology to empower the subject in his or her historical social conditions, and not in an abstract subjectivity" (Schuster and Boschert-Kimmig, 1999: 24).

The articulation between the collective and the individual becomes visible in the way progressive Islamic theologies deal with the struggle for women's rights. According to said theologies, the criteria for identifying "progressive Muslims" implies precisely "striv[ing] to realize a just and pluralistic society through critically engaging Islam, a relentless pursuit of social justice, an emphasis on gender equality as a foundation of human rights, a vision of religious and ethnic pluralism, and a methodology of nonviolent resistance" (Safi, 2005, cit. in: Duderija, 2010: 412).

Multiple dimensions of unjust human suffering

According to progressive political theologies, God is involved in the history of oppressed peoples and in their struggles for liberation. In the case of Christian theologies, the story of Jesus shows how God becomes poor and powerless so that the oppressed may liberate themselves from poverty and powerlessness, and the resurrection of Jesus is just a metaphor for the freedom to struggle against oppression. Regarding progressive Islamic theologies, for instance, the starting point is the Qur'anic statement that "Allah does not oppress," a statement that encourages Amina Wadud to state the following: "I consider myself a believing Muslim who works for justice *on the basis of my faith*. I consider myself a pro-faith, pro-feminist Muslim woman" (2006: 4). Theologies differ according to the specific people, social group, or type of suffering they privilege. Multiple dimensions of concrete unjust human suffering are thereby revealed, opening up a broad and dense landscape of oppressive relations and struggles for justice that fly in the face of any reductionist theory of history or social emancipation. A few examples will suffice to illustrate this point.

The first generation of Latin American liberation theologies were concerned with morally repugnant social inequality. They focused their attention on the poor and excluded, such as peasants and landless rural workers, unemployed or miserably paid industrial workers, miners, the new slave workers of neocolonial plantations laboring under the most subhuman conditions, or squatter settlers.[1] In the following years, other forms of oppression, such as sexual discrimination against women, were included in the theological reflection and practice, thus giving rise to a vibrant current of feminist theologies in Latin America and elsewhere.[2] The importance of feminist liberation theologies cannot be overemphasized, since all major religions discriminate against women. Feminist liberation theologies developed areas of concern that had been neglected by male liberation theologians. According to Rosemary Ruether, those areas include: the question of culture and spirituality—the elements of personal nurture and supportive community often ignored in favor of social action (Aquino, 1996; Pereira, 2002; Marcos, 2002; Ville, 2012); a new conception of the human-nature relationship that interconnects ecological distortion and social injustice (Ress, 2006; Gebara, 1998); the focus on women-church, that is, small intentional communities, usually women, who gather for mutual support and consciousness-raising and who collaborate with other social movements inside and outside the church;[3] a comprehensive transformation of interpersonal and social relations that aim at the simultaneous transformation of males and females;[4] and the recognition of the interconnection in social systems of various kinds of oppression—gender, social class, race—leading to an inclusive vision of liberation, not simply a vision aimed at one group leaving some other oppression intact (Ruether, 1991: 228–29).[5]

Since the 1970s, the internal differentiation of feminist theologies has followed a similar development occurring in secular feminism (white, black, middle class, Third World, *mujerista*, lesbian, indigenous, *mestiza/o* feminism). The fragmentation of feminist activism deriving from such subcoding has led Margaret Kamitsuka, who calls herself a "white feminist theologian," to argue recently that "it would be valuable to be able to recuperate 'feminist theology' as an overtly neutral, noncoded term that can, at certain times, be used to refer to the diversity of these and other yet-to-be-named women's theological writings (with care always taken by hegemonic positionalities to self-name)" (2004: 179).

The awareness of persisting colonial relations in supposedly postcolonial states brought the question of colonialism and racism to the center of theological analysis. Accordingly, the suffering and struggles of indigenous peoples, the most distinctive victims of racist white Christianity, led to a new perspective in liberation theology—indigenous theology—anchored either in Christianity or in indigenous religions and spirituality. A related perspective on Latin American liberation theology developed from the historical experience of poverty and discrimination by Chicanos, *la Raza, mestizos,* and other offspring of the indigenous women whom the Spanish conquistadores raped or took as wives. A Chicano liberation theology thus emerged, and, in some versions, the notion of *La Raza Cosmica* is articulated with the symbolic role of *Nuestra Señora de Guadalupe* (Guerrero, 1987).[6] Postcolonial criticism in feminist theologies is also present in Islamic feminisms, namely as regards the polemics over the *niqab* and the burqa. As Barlas comments thus on the prohibition of the burqa in the Netherlands: "The *burqa*, it seems, can be deployed to justify both annihilating and assimilating Muslims in the name of Western universalism. This spectrum, of annihilation/assimilation, is a legacy of the 'discovery' of the Americas when Anglo-Europeans were confronted with the problem of the other in the form of Amerindians and the challenge of making sense of difference" (2006: 9).

In the late 1960s, the civic rights and black power movements in the USA gained a theological component through the groundbreaking work of the African American theologian James Cone (1969). According to Cone, the Jesus of white European and American Christianity had very little to say to the millions of African Americans deprived of basic rights and living in hunger and despair only because a white supremacist society had declared them inferior and unworthy. For Cone (1972), the central theological concept in the black spirituals is the divine liberation of the oppressed from slavery. The denunciation of racism as being incompatible with the idea of a righteous God gave rise to a new perspective in liberation theology: black theology.[7]

Ethnic and religious discrimination and oppression, as well as the unjust human suffering they have caused throughout history, constitute another major topic of progressive theologies. In Judaism, the historical Jewish suffering culminating in the horror of the holocaust is the central theme of theological reflection. Mark Ellis, one of the most eloquent expounders of Jewish liberation theology, has noted that contemporary Jewish theology displays an intriguing lack of interest in liberation theology, all the more intriguing, in fact, since the Exodus, as the narrative of the liberation of the Jewish people and the prophetic tradition that it started, is very much present in Christian liberation theologies. Here is Ellis's explanation for this phenomenon:

> The recently empowered contemporary Jewish community . . . appears fearful—and perhaps threatened—by such a prophetic revival within Christianity, for, in its use of the Exodus and the prophets, Christian liberation theologies speak for those on the underside of history, the marginalized and the oppressed. The Jewish tradition is atrophying under the mantle of political empowerment"(2004: 145).

This explanation seems to be substantiated by the emergence of a Palestinian-Christian liberation theology, which, although speaking for a tiny religious minority in the region, represents an important theological reflection by Arab and Palestinian Christians on the oppression of the Palestinian people and on their oppressors, Zionism and the state of Israel.[8] Recognizing that the impetus for Zionism has been the history of violent Western anti-Semitism, Palestinian liberation theologians speak of the transference of the sin from West to East: ascribing to the innocent population of Palestine the expiation of a crime committed by Western Christians. "Because the Christians of Europe and America denied their responsibility for a million Jews who were their brothers, they threw one million Arabs out of their homeland of Palestine" (Ellis, 2004: 153). From the Balfour declaration of 1917 to the founding of the state of Israel in 1948 from the 1967 war to the subsequent tragic unfolding of the Israel-Palestine conflict ever since, an unjust suffering and humiliation has been imposed on the Palestinian people with the complicity of Western Christianity. Herein lies the core of Palestinian liberation theology, of which one of the leading representatives is Naim Ateek. His book, *Justice, and Only Justice: A Palestinian Theology of Liberation,* was published in 1989 in response to the first uprising. According to Ateek, the history of the suffering of the Jews in Europe is a prelude to Zionist colonization and the occupation of Palestine. Indeed, his personal account of the occupation by Jewish soldiers of his hometown, Beisan, twenty miles south of the Sea of Galilee, bears disturbing similarities to what happened just two decades earlier to the Jews of Eastern and Central Europe (1989: 7–13). Palestinian liberation theology has a specific interest in the biblical message and in finding there a path for Palestinians and Jews beyond opposition and destruction. Says Ateek: "God has something very relevant and very important to say to both the oppressed and the oppressors in the Middle East" (1989: 6).[9] On the question of the Holocaust, he formulates the principle that should ground the road to a mutually honorable peace: "We must understand the importance and significance of the Holocaust to the Jews, while insisting that the Jews understand the importance and significance of the tragedy of Palestine for the Palestinians" (1989: 168). Jonathan Kuttab, in turn, calls attention to the critical potential of the notion of the "rule of law" in the Old Testament: limiting the powers of the rulers on the basis of the recognition that God is the only lord of the universe. The fact that the governments of Israel yielded to the "idolatry of national security" (1992: 95) led the Palestinians to assume the role of the prophets of the Old Testament, providing the critical voice and action vis-à-vis such idolatry. Mitri Raheb (1995) argues that, in view of the situation confronting the Palestinians, Christians must not remain neutral; rather, they should place themselves on the side of the oppressed. And Munir Fasheh asserts: "we have to declare, as Christian Arabs, that we are not a part of the Christianity that helped plunder five continents, enslave people in many regions, and wipe out people and civilizations in North America and Australia, and is now threatening the Palestinians with a similar fate" (1992: 67).

Christian Arabs and Palestinians are a minority, which in itself constitutes another factor of discrimination and unjust human suffering. This fact comes out very vividly in another perspective of liberation theology developed by Christians in Korea. A Korean word, *minjung,* meaning "people," has given its name to this theology. Minjung theology focuses on the oppression of Korean Christians under the dictatorial regimes that ruled the country for more than three decades. In the words of one of its most distinguished representatives, Suh Kwang-Sun David:

> [The] theology of minjung is a creation of those Christians who were forced to reflect upon their Christian discipleship in basement interrogation rooms, in trials, facing court martial tribunals, hearing the allegations of prosecutors, . . . house arrest and twenty-four-hour watch over their activities . . . . Korean Christians want to speak of what they have learned and reflected upon theologically and to share this with others who in their own social and political context are searching for a relevant theology in Asia. (1983: 16)[10]

Within Christianity, another form of unjust human suffering that has been the object of theological reflection and progressive religious activism is the caste system and, in particular, the plight of the Dalits, also called "untouchables," in India. The Dalits are around 20 percent of the population of India and, despite the laws that prohibit discriminatory practices on the basis of caste, they are still today denied the most basic human rights and are discriminated against in their access to jobs, education, public facilities, Hindu temples, and, sometimes, even water. According to their leaders, they live in a situation of apartheid. The theological reflection on their oppression and liberation has given rise to a Dalit liberation theology (Irudayaraj, 1990).

Without any pretension to being exhaustive,[11] I have briefly presented some perspectives on liberation theology as illustrations of the ways in which theological reflection and the religious practices it is associated with get involved in the struggles for progressive social transformation. Liberation theologies are socially and culturally contextualized in such a way as to contribute to raising the critical awareness of concrete peoples, oppressed by concrete forms of unequal power relations. In so doing, they may contribute to empower people to change existing values and relationships.

Suffering of the flesh

The trivialization of human suffering in our time and the consequent indifference with which we face the other's suffering—even if its presence in our senses is overwhelming—has many causes. Relevant factors are, no doubt, the impact of the society of information and communication—the repetition of visibility without the visibility of repetition—and the aversion to suffering induced by its medicalization. However, at a deeper level, the trivialization of suffering resides in the categories we use to classify and organize it, whereas the truth is that suffering is, above all, a declassifying and deorganizing of the body. The modern Western cultural tradition, by separating the soul from the body, degraded the latter, particularly for being constituted by human flesh. As a consequence, the conceptualization (and dignification) of human suffering was brought about by abstract categories, whether philosophical or ethical, that devalue the visceral dimension of suffering, its visible mark of experience lived in the flesh.[12]

This process of disembodying through classification and organization is present even in the authors that most claimed the importance of the place of the body, from Nietzsche to Foucault and Levinas, to mention only a few. For the same reason, with the exception of sight—always privileged by modernity as an instrument of representation—our senses were desensitized for the direct experience of the suffering of others and even of one's own suffering. The flesh, both the flesh of pleasure and the flesh of suffering, was thus deprived of its bodily materiality, and hence of the instinctive and affective reactions that it can provoke, whose intensity lies in their being beyond words, beyond reasonable argument or reflective evaluation.

Religions and theologies were not immune to this biopolitical device. As they followed it, however, they revealed its limits and contradictions. On the one hand, they pushed to extremes the repulsion of the flesh as a site of pleasure, always associating it with sex and women. On the other hand, they incited believers to succor the neighbor's body with no other mediation than compassion. They thus allowed for a direct, dense, and intense access to suffering flesh, that was completely different from the access made possible by medical science, an access made of epistemological (subject/object), categorial, and professional distances. It is, moreover, a practical access that, unlike medical access, does not seek a balance between understanding and intervention. It gives absolute priority to intervention, to the detriment of understanding.

Such are the reasons why religions have allowed for the creation of ethics of care and engagement based on visceral reactions of intersubjectivity between self and neighbor, engagements that are prerepresentational and even preethical, made up of sensibilities and availabilities that need no arguments or rules to be strong and self-evident. The underside of this immediacy of suffering is its depoliticization. This is precisely what happened with the most emblematic case of suffering flesh in one of the monotheist religions, Catholicism: the crucifixion of Jesus Christ. The highly political nature of this suffering seems to have been sequestered by the theology of resurrection; that is to say, by a flight from the world, a flight that, unlike Allah's journey to heaven, had no return. The historical figure of Jesus is also relevant for Islam. Obviously, the Jesus of the Christian Gospels is different from the Jesus of the Qur'an and the Islamic tradition (Khalidi, 2001). The difference has much to do with the suffering of the flesh. While for the Christians what really matters is Jesus' own flesh and its suffering, since he is the "Word made flesh," for the Islamic faith Jesus is an example of piety because of his proximity to the suffering of the flesh of others, feeding the hungry, healing the sick, restoring life. As Ayoub writes: "Jesus the 'Christ', the 'eternal logos', the 'Word made flesh', the 'Only Begotten Son of God' and second person of trinity has been the barrier separating the two communities and long obscuring the meaning and significance of Jesus, the 'Word of God' to Muslim faith and theology" (1995: 65).

The counterhegemonic potential of progressive theologies resides in the articulation they strive for between the visceral engagement in a succoring gesture or nonconditioned care, and the political struggle against the causes of suffering as part of the unfinished task of divinity. In his critique of secularism as a veiled form of restrictive pluralism (for excluding religion as a legitimate way of being), William Connolly speaks of "visceral registers of subjectivity and inter-subjectivity" (1999: 11) as an expression of very intense experiences, carrying unsuspected energies for existential fulfillment. As an example, he offers the registers of religious subjectivity (1999: 27). There is, thus, a connection between visceral intersubjectivity and radical will, which I analyze in the next section.

An insurgent radical will and a postcapitalist horizon

Institutionalized religion paid a high price to find a modus vivendi with Western modernity and the Enlightenment: privatization. But moving into the private sphere had a contradictory effect. On the one hand, religion was banished from the political system (which, however, as I mentioned above, did not mean rendering the church incapable of interfering in politics), but, on the other hand, it was left on its own, more or less self-regulated in the private sphere. This means that within the private sphere religion could keep a kind of premodern or transmodern radical engagement with the lives of people, both in terms of discourses and in terms of practices, an engagement that was free from the political, cultural, discursive, and institutional mediations that other (secular) social mobilizations in the public sphere went through in the last two centuries, most notably the labor movement and the feminist movement.

This explains, in part at least, why the religious mobilizations reclaiming the public sphere in our time are endowed with a kind of radicalness that we cannot find in most social movements. This radical energy is used by traditionalist theologies to turn the clock back to a time in which religious institutions controlled social and political hierarchies; but it has also been used by pluralist, progressive theologies to struggle against all such hierarchies and the oppressions and discriminations they generate. While the former theologies seek to attain power over an unjust and oppressive public sphere, and will certainly end up making it even more unjust and oppressive, the latter fight against power, injustice, and oppression, whether occurring in the public or private sphere, and regardless of its causes, including the religious ones.

The link between theology and a radical critique of capitalism is at the core of liberation theologies. As Gutiérrez says: "the potential of a liberating faith lies in the revolutionary capacity to change the concrete life of the poor and oppressed peoples . . . political radicalness and evangelical radicalness meet and reinforce each other" (2004: 37–38). Jürgen Moltmann, one of the representatives of the progressive political theologies, asks: "how can I live with any decency at all as a member of the 'First World' in the face of the Third?" (1982: 155). In a different but related sense, he speaks of "progressive revelation" as the manifestation of a link between the Christian spirit and the spirit of a modern age that "produces progressively better views of the world and of life" (1967: 225). The progress of human society is thus interpreted as the self-movement of revelation. Similarly, Ignacio Ellacuría states that the history of salvation is historical salvation, that is, historical fulfillment in society (1977: 130). Reclaiming the need for a theological Third World perspective informed by Marxism and the theory of dependence, Ellacuría affirms: "it is impossible to see the achievement of justice without a basic revolution in the social and economic order, or a true fulfillment of man without bringing an adequate economic structure into operation" (1977: 127).

For progressive political theologies, liberation rather than resistance or salvation grounds the radical will to struggle for a more just society. According to Dorothee Soelle,

Resistance . . . is how human beings who are members of the white bourgeoisie—those who normally participate in oppression and profit from exploitation—participate in liberation struggles . . . . Whereas salvation is the deed of a totally other, who deals with unsaved people to save them, liberation is cooperation between Christ and the people . . . . Nobody can give liberation to someone

else . . . . The liberator is expression and part of the movement of liberation . . . .
To participate in the struggle is a necessary presupposition of the concept of
liberation. (2006: 141)

The impulse for interculturality in the struggles for human dignity

As I mentioned above, the conventional and by far dominant conceptions and
practices of human rights are monocultural, and this constitutes one of the major obstacles to building a real, bottom-up universal struggle for human rights.
Religion, on the contrary, exists only as an immense diversity of religions, both
as diversity among major religions and as diversity within each religion.[13] In the
Western metropolitan world this diversity was probably one of the unintended
consequences of the privatization of religion. As I have argued elsewhere (Santos, 1995), the three principles of social regulation of Western modernity are
the state, the market, and the community. In the last two hundred years, the
principle of the state and the principle of the market have been disputing prece-
dence in social regulation (in our time, neoliberalism is premised upon the pre-
cedence of the market). All along, the third principle, the community, has been
neglected, always conceived of, at best, as adjuvant to the state or the market.
This neglect allowed the principle of the community to evolve unencumbered
by bureaucratic or market standardization and thus in a much less monocultural and monolithic manner. Expelled from the state and the market, religion
took refuge in the community, a domain of social regulation less standardized
and more open to diversity.

In spite of the setbacks and shortcomings (discretionary selectivity, temp-
tation to claim a single revealed truth, lack of practical consequences), the
ecumenical and interreligious dialogues bear witness to a potential for interculturality within the domain of religion. If more coherently and actively pursued, such dialogues may be both a powerful memory and a tested training
ground for broader dialogues involving religious and nonreligious conceptions
of human dignity. In recent times there have been some courageous attempts at
such dialogues from within the most intractable political conditions. Two examples among many: in the Middle East, the contributions of Naim Ateek and
Mark Ellis, in particular the latter's "Four Elements of a Jewish Response" to
Christian liberation theologies (2004: 163–202); in India, the name of Asghar
Ali Engineer (1998) comes to mind, the Islamic intellectual and movement
leader, champion of a much-needed dialogue between Islam and Hinduism.
In some countries, such as Pakistan and Israel, intrafaith dialogues are as in-

tractable and as full of consequences as the interfaith dialogues. In the case of Pakistan, the work of Fazlur Rahman (1982, 2000) is particularly eloquent in this respect.

Far beyond inter-religious dialogues, religious thinkers in general have oscillated between strict dogmatism and orthodoxy, on one side, and the vibrant questioning of texts, practices, rules, and institutions, on the other. In the latter case they have often risked heresy and suffered drastic consequences because they go beyond familiar religious materials, drawing on strange cultures and different knowledges and philosophies, or immerse themselves in the delights of everyday experiences and discourses by mingling with merchants, artisans, and prostitutes and deriving momentous theoretical consequences from such experiences and discourses. In other words, when they decide to go at their own risk to the roots of established truths, religious thinkers tend to be greater *bricoleurs* than any other thinkers, combining in innovative and chaotic ways fragments from different provenances, and on that basis offering new meanings and interpretations. In order to do so they adopt epistemologies that in contemporary terms we would consider positional or situated knowledge. They excel in occupying the contact zones among different cultures and ways of knowing, borderlines, thresholds, *nepantlism* (the Aztec word for "torn between ways"), twilight zones neither outside nor inside, neither familiar nor foreign, neither subject nor object, conditions of exile without ceasing to be an insider. In a sense, they anticipate the epistemological in-betweenness without which intercultural exchanges cannot be successfully accomplished.

In all religious traditions we find such thinkers. In the Christian tradition, Augustine and Nicolas of Cusa come to mind, or Ghazali in Islam. The latter has come to our attention thanks to the masterful work of Ebrahim Moosa (2005). According to Moosa, Ghazali—a towering Islamic intellectual of Persian origin who lived in the eleventh and twelfth centuries CE—drew on the most diverse Islamic and non-Islamic sources, from the Hebrew Bible to Greek philosophy, from experiences gained through travel to mystical experiences. He saw himself occupying a threshold position, in the *dihiliz*, a Persian word that designates the in-between space between the street and the inside of the house. When seen from the street, the *dihiliz* is an inside; when viewed from inside the house, it is an outside (2005: 45). This explains why, in such a space, Ghazali could simultaneously feel himself both in exile and at home inside his own house.[14] The Catholic theologian Raimundo Panikkar, who in his upbringing carries Hindu traditions as well, may also be considered an example of a theologian and thinker "occupying a threshold position": he cultivated a Christian thought with a Hindu expression. In his point of view, Christianity, in order to be truly Christian, "to belong to the entire world," should discard the Western, colonial robes that pretended that Christianity is only viable through Western culture. Hence, his question: "Is it possible for us to admit that there are limits to the understanding of God we received from the Semitic and Greco-Roman traditions? Can we admit that there are also limits to our understanding of religion . . . and prayer . . . ?" (Panikkar, 2011).

The narratives of suffering and liberation

The privileged language of intercultural exchange is the narrative. Storytelling generates a sense of immediate and concrete copresence through which social experiences existing in different times, spaces, and cultures become more easily accessible and intelligible, a type of copresence that cannot be achieved by conceptual language (whether technical, philosophical, or scientific). The narrative, even when it is a historical narrative, works against time by producing an effect of synchronicity and contemporaneity that helps to convert the stranger into the familiar and the remote into the coeval. Moreover, the world's *memoria passionis* (a Jewish and Christian category) lies in remembrance and narratives that, by recounting exemplary struggles of life and death, suffering and liberation, loss and gain, reinforce sentiments of joy and fear, awe and wonder, revenge and compassion, from which a kind of bottom-up shared wisdom of the world emerges. Contrary to historical reconstruction, the *memoria passionis* collapses past, present, and future together; it sees strengths in weaknesses and alternative possibilities in defeats.[15] The wisdom it gives rise to is as contemplative as it is active; it is a global storehouse of remembrance and vision that converts the past into an energy to empower the present and strengthen the *not yet* or the *perhaps* of the future. Moreover, narratives, stories, and parables are open-ended. They offer themselves to reinterpretation and contextualization and in this sense allow for a continuous reinvention of authorship or coauthorship. Storytellers are always coauthors of the stories they heard from their predecessors.

I see here the possibility for another fruitful encounter between human rights and progressive political theologies. Narration and storytelling lie at the foundation of religious experience, be they based on sacred texts or sacred oral traditions. Moreover, even religious philosophy, dogmatics, and exegesis are sustainable only if grounded on the exemplary events, sayings, and concrete lives of concrete persons and peoples—whether extraordinary or ordinary, but never anonymous. They operate through an extremely extended case method, as we might call it, a method that allows for the establishment of a logical connection between the most localized, specific, and even unique circumstances and the most far-reaching, general, transpacial and transtemporal consequences and relevance. In parallel interviews, both Johann Baptist Metz and Elie Wiesel underline the central role of the narrative in religious thinking (Schuster and Boschert-Kimmig, 1999). As Elie Wiesel says: "Theology is nothing other than telling stories" (1999: 94). All the prophets spoke in parables with an eye on later believers and their reinterpretations in light of their own experiences and their own intellectual freedom. In the words of Moosa: "Texts and interpretations are, in the final instance, stories about events. . . . Narrative is not the verbal and literal repetition of stories; the purpose of the latter is in their substance and meanings. What is unique about narrative is its ability to tell the past event as if it were occurring in the present—namely at the time of speaking" (2005: 67).

The conventional nature of human rights discourse resides not only in a certain complicit promiscuity between the abstract proclamation of human rights and resignation before their systematic violations, but also and mainly in the trivialization of the human suffering entailed by such violations. Such trivialization results to a large extent from the normalized discourse (Foucault, 1976, 1977, 1980) of the organizations for the defense of human rights and its strong statistical component, which reduces to the anonymity of numbers the horror of human degradation and unjust suffering. The destabilizing presence of suffering is thus neutralized, and thereby loses the possibility of grounding the radical will and the militancy to fight against the state of affairs that produces unjust suffering in a systematic way. By insisting on the concrete narrative of the victims' suffering and their struggle against oppression, progressive political theologies may contribute to turn unjust suffering into an intolerable presence dehumanizing both the victims and the oppressors, as well as all those who, feeling themselves neither victims nor oppressors, consider unjust suffering a problem that does not concern them.

The presence of the world before or beyond interpretation

The intercultural conception of human rights for which I have been pleading (Santos, 2007c: 3–40) seeks to strengthen the legitimacy of both a worldwide and a place-based politics of human rights and to radicalize the struggles that can be undertaken in its name. The notion of interculturality is meant to convey the idea that the focus of intercultural exchanges is interpretation, the production and sharing of meaning. I have already suggested that meaning does not necessarily involve conceptual language and that narrative and storytelling may be even more powerful tools to make social experiences separated by time, space, and culture mutually accessible, intelligible, and relevant. It is, however, necessary to go beyond this and to show that, if an ecology of different conceptions of human dignity is to ground a more encompassing and radical struggle for human dignity, it will presuppose the creation of particularly intense moments of copresence, moments in which presence precedes meaning.

Presence is the thingness or materiality upon which meanings are built. It refers to bodies, signs, sounds, and materials in their nonsemantic capacity, that is, in their direct or immediate access to our senses. It is a form of being that, as Hans Ulrich Gumbrecht rightly states, "refers to the things of the world before they become part of a culture" (2004: 70). It is through meaning that things become culturally specific and often also incommensurable or unintelligible to other cultures. In my view, such "things" are not outside a culture; they are rather inside but in a different, noncultural way. They have a prerepresentational capacity of being outside thought and consciousness, while grounding thought and consciousness. They are material and operate at the level of instinct, emotion, and affect. As Nietzsche's Zarathustra ([1883] 2012: 19) puts it, "Behind thy thoughts and feelings, my brother, there is a mighty lord, an unknown sage—it is called Self; it dwelleth in thy body, it is thy body. There is more sagacity in thy body than in thy best wisdom."

Of the authors that have drawn our attention to the nonsemantic dimension of interaction and communication, Gumbrecht is the most eloquent in counterposing cultures that are ridden by presence (presence-cultures) and cultures that are ridden by meaning (meaning-cultures) (2004: 79). Of course, in all cultures there is presence and meaning, but the emphasis on one or the other varies across cultures. Modern Western culture is a meaning-culture, while medieval Western culture was a presence-culture.[16] I suggest that some non-Western cultures are best understood as presence-cultures.

In intercultural exchanges specifically, the role of presence is to propitiate the generation of senses of commonality, of culturally indifferent diversity, and of immediate evidence. A bundle of mutilated bodies in a killing field; the skinny body of a child about to die of hunger; the cry of a woman over the dead body of her young son; the sight of a naked body; an ecstatic movement or posture; the body's movements; the smells, instruments, and ingredients in the performance of a ritual, all these presences are endowed with a power that seems relatively autonomous in relation to the meanings that may be attributed to them.

This is not the place to discuss the possible role of a dialectics of interpretation and presence in the construction of new intercultural transformative thinking and practice. At this juncture, I just want to underline the fact that here, too, I see a possible contribution of progressive religious experience and theological reflexivity to strengthen, expand, and radicalize human rights struggles. The presentification of the past or of the Other through rites, rituals, and sacraments (for instance, the Eucharist, particularly in Catholicism) plays a central role in religious experience (Asad, 1993). The same immediate evidence that overcomes strangeness and difference is present in particular types of religious experience: mysticism in Christianity, Kabbalah in Judaism, Sufism in Islam, the Possession of the Pai-de-Santo or Mãe-de-Santo in *Umbanda* or *Candomblé*, and so forth. An intensified sense of sharing and of belonging is thereby generated that, if put at the service of struggles of resistance and liberation from oppression, may contribute to strengthen and radicalize the will for social transformation. It is not by proselytistic caprice or excessive zeal that all the meetings, rallies, protests, and land occupations organized by one of the most important social movements of our time—O Movimento dos Sem Terra (MST; the Movement of the Landless Rural Workers in Brazil)—start with what they call the *mística*, a moment of silence, prayer, and singing, the militants hand in hand in a circle, individual physical bodies becoming a collective physical body.

Songs and chants have historically been a very strong presence in struggles of resistance and liberation as a way of gathering strength to overcome despair and gain courage to fight against formidable oppressors. Presence through songs and chants is a way of transcending the body without ever leaving it, of transcending differences for the sake of the harmony needed for a practical task at hand (which may be the singing itself or something beyond it), of constructing material strength out of symbolic strength. Here, again, the religions of the oppressed and the liberation theologies they have given rise to in recent times bear a precious historical experience through which human rights may gain new voices and new vitalities and new strengths. Blues and spirituals play an important role in black theology. Other examples may be found in the way the Caribbean theology of decolonization uses Bob Marley's redemptive songs (Erskine, 1998) or the way the liberation theology of indigenous or tribal people of Northeast India emphasizes a specific doxology: the practice of praising God through singing and dancing (Thanzauva, 2002: 269).

The spirituality of/in material struggles for social transformation

We should be aware that the distinction between the material and the spiritual is a Western-based distinction. In their analyses of epistemology and religion in Africa, Stephen Ellis and Gerrie Haar forcefully argue that the existing models of the relationship between religion and politics are based on the assumption of a structural distinction between the visible or material world and the invisible world, whereas such a rigid distinction does not reflect ideas about the nature of reality that are prevalent in Africa. According to them, among the most salient features of African epistemologies is a conviction that the material and immaterial aspects of life cannot be separated, although they can be distinguished from each other, much as the two sides of a coin can be discerned but not parted. They believe in the existence of an invisible world, distinct but not separate from the visible one, that is home to spiritual beings with effective powers over the material world (2007: 387).

This cautionary note may help us to have a deeper understanding of counter-hegemonic human rights struggles. Such struggles aim at changing the social structures that are accountable for systemically produced unjust human suffering. They are material struggles in the sense that their political impetus must address the political economy underlying the production and reproduction of unequal social relations, even of those relations that are less directly or less linearly connected with capitalist exploitation and class-based hierarchy, such as those usually dealt with by conventional identity politics. They are also material in the sense that they presuppose political, financial, and human resources to build organizations and generate militancy. But beyond all that, counter-hegemonic human rights struggles are very often high-risk, sometimes life-threatening struggles against very powerful and unscrupulous enemies. They have, therefore, to be grounded on strongly motivated political will, a will that has to be both collective and individual, since there is no collective activism without individual activists. Without a nonconformist, rebellious, insurgent will, no meaningful social struggles against institutionalized injustice and oppression can succeed.

No such will may be formed without both radical and destabilizing critical visions of current injustice and credible visions of an alternative, better society. In the last two centuries, two very strong and credible visions of an alternative society dominated: socialism and national liberation from colonialism. They were related to two equally strong critical visions of contemporary societies: the anticapitalist critique and the anticolonial critique. For reasons I cannot go into here, these visions entered into crisis in the course of the last thirty years, and these crises are the other side of the current ideological and political inter-regnum in the strong struggles for progressive social transformation. Modern secularism prevented religion from having any significant participation in these visions. At least in the Christian world, institutionalized religion made peace with the power structures of the day no matter how unjust, it hijacked the motivational strength contained in spirituality,[17] and it turned believers into individual seekers of individual salvation in afterlife worlds. It was this type of religion that Marx so rightly criticized.

In our time, and as I have been arguing in this chapter, progressive political theologies have used the critique of the modern privatization of religion to develop new conceptions of salvation and redemption that might ground the struggles for social transformation, justice, and liberation. For such theologies, turning to God amounts to turning to a neighbor when in need. In doing so, they opened the possibility of releasing in society a new energy, "infusing" social struggles with the motivational strength contained in spirituality. This explains in part why in the last forty years so many human rights activists who paid with their lives for their commitment to struggles for social justice were disciples of liberation theology in one of its many versions.

As a concrete experience of religiosity, spirituality has many different forms, and in any major religion different forms have predominated in different historical and geographical contexts. For instance, in Christianity, in the context of the persecution that occurred before the Roman emperor Constantine was converted, martyrdom was considered the ideal or highest form of testimony, testimony being considered the Christian form of spirituality. Many Christians viewed their death as the "baptismal of blood" or as a "second baptism," and it was celebrated as their heavenly birthday. It was also regarded as an imitation of Jesus Christ, who laid down his life (Thanzauva, 2002: 256).[18] Martyrdom is not a thing of the past, as illustrated by the deaths of Martin Luther King, Jr., or D. Oscar Romero, archbishop of El Salvador, as well as by the deaths of so many anonymous believers whose sacrifices never hit the news. As Thanzauva says: "Today in India, many Christians have lost their lives, properties and suffered persecution for no other sin except they are Christians" (2002: 256). Moreover, martyrdom is present in all major religions.[19]

Some forms of spirituality are favored by traditionalist theologies, as defined above, and are of little use for the kind of counterhegemonic human rights struggles I have been arguing for in this book, while others are favored by pluralist and progressive theologies and have the potential to contribute to such struggles. The intensity of the spiritual experience matters, but what matters most is its existential orientation. Is it experienced as an individual achievement without any relevant connection to the affairs of this world, or, on the contrary, as a way of sharing with others a transcendental vision of a suffering God that is manifest in the suffering peoples of this unjust world?[20] In the first case we may find highly intense forms of spirituality, but their intensity is precisely measured by their capacity to withdraw from this world. This is, in general, the case with mystics. The strong potential of mysticism for presence, referred to above, is neutralized by the possessive individualism[21] of the "mystic union" with the Absolute.[22] In the second case, spirituality generates a powerful motivational energy that, if channeled toward progressive struggles for social justice, will reinforce the credibility of the visions that guide activists and strengthen their will. This has been most prominently the case of the base ecclesial communities in Latin America inspired by liberation theology (Boff, 1986).

IN THIS BOOK I have pursued a twofold objective: to identify the major challenges that the rise of political theologies at the beginning of the twenty-first century have posed to human rights, and to select within a broad landscape of theological analysis the types of reflections and practices that might contribute to expand and deepen the canon of human rights politics. In order to achieve this double goal I have used complexity as my main analytical guideline. This has led me to make distinctions from which significant consequences have been drawn: on one side, distinctions between different types of political theologies (pluralist versus fundamentalist; traditionalist versus progressive); on the other, distinctions between two contrasting discourses and practices of human rights politics (hegemonic versus counterhegemonic). I have also argued that pluralist and progressive theologies may be a source of radical energy for counterhegemonic human rights struggles.

I am assuming that the distinctions between theologies apply, with certain nuances, to all major religions. This is an assumption whose warranty I cannot fully vouch for. It derives less from theological hermeneutics than from witnessing how religious people and practices position themselves in social struggles. Which side are they on? This is my basic criterion. On the side of the oppressors, or on the side of the oppressed? On the side of fundamentalism, or on the side of pluralism? On the side of reactionary traditionalism, or on the side of progressive social transformation (which does not exclude recourse to tradition, as indigenous and Islamic liberation theology illustrates)?

I am well aware that it may be difficult in many circumstances to answer these questions unequivocally. The major difficulty has to do with the role religion plays in society. The context varies according to the different religions and historical periods. One of the most eloquent statements concerning the need to take account of contexts in this regard is by Ali Shariati in a talk he delivered in the 1970s:

> Franz Fanon, whom I knew personally and whose books I translated into Persian, was pessimistic about the positive contribution of religion to social movement. He had, in fact, an anti-religious attitude, until I convinced him that in some societies where religion plays an important role in the culture, religion can, through its resources and psychological effects, help the enlightened person to lead his [or her] society toward the same destination toward which Fanon was taking his own through non-religious means. I added further that Fanon's anti-religious feeling stemmed from the unique religious experience of Europe in the Middle Ages and the ensuing freedom of European society in the fifteenth and sixteenth centuries. One cannot extend this experience to the Islamic world, because the culture of an Islamic society and the tradition that has shaped Islamic societies is utterly different from the spirit that under the name of religion ruled Europe in the Middle Ages. Logically, therefore, one cannot judge and condemn both religions on the same ground. A comparison between the role of Islam in Africa and that of Christianity in Latin America illustrates my point. (2002: 36)

I also think that the last several decades have offered us a variety of social experiences providing some clues for tentative answers in concrete situations. For instance, in the World Social Forum, whose unfolding I have analyzed (Santos, 2006b), I have witnessed the presence of activists in social struggles for socioeconomic, historical, sexual, racial, cultural, and postcolonial justice who base their activism and their claims on Christian, Islamic, Judaic, Hindu, Buddhist, and indigenous religious beliefs and spiritualities. In a sense, they bear witness to a political intersubjectivity that seems to have deserted conventional secular critical thinking and political action: the combination of creative effervescence and intense and passionate energy, on one side, with a pluralistic, open-ended, and nonviolent conception of struggle, on the other.

As I have said, I took for granted in this book that all religions have, in principle, the same potential to develop progressive, liberationist versions of theologies capable of inserting themselves in counterhegemonic struggles against neoliberal globalization. Conversely, all religions have an impressive record of executions, persecutions, pogroms, and burned books. A related issue, which

I did not treat in this book, concerns the reasons why the economic, social, political, and cultural conditions prevailing in the world today are particularly effective in preventing the emergence of liberation theologies and in promoting the emergence of conservative or reactionary ones. In this context, it makes sense to quote Ali Shariati one more time, as his views drive home the dangers religion could bring to the struggle for social emancipation. As he concludes his talk, Shariati identifies the perils an enlightened Muslim must face:

> An enlightened person should be aware that the deviant and reactionary elements that have always been against the masses and have always played with their destiny and exploited them, have been misusing religion as an effective weapon to divert the feelings and the attention of the masses from their present affairs and make them think about past problems only. They divert people's attention from the present as well as the actual and material problems while, in the name of religion keeping the people preoccupied with the afterlife as well as abstract and subjective issues, so that Muslims are prevented from striving for a comfortable, affluent, and free life, Even their ideals and thinking regarding these matters are focused on the hereafter. As a result, religion, which had been the greatest source of energy and aspiration and the guide to a meaningful life on earth, becomes distorted to such an extent that the eyes, ears and hearts of its followers are focused on the hereafter. Paying attention to life on this earth is considered a source of corruption while mysticism and eschatology are greatly encouraged. (2002:46)

The main idea behind this inquiry is that we live in a time in which the most appalling social injustices and unjust human sufferings no longer seem to generate the moral indignation and political will needed both to combat them effectively and to create a more just and fair society. Under such circumstances, it seems evident that we cannot afford to waste any genuine social experience that we might resort to in order to strengthen the organization and the determination of all those who have not given up the struggle for a better society, and specifically those who have done so under the banner of human rights. Not to waste social experience means also to recycle and transform it in light of the objectives at hand. Such a work of transformation was undertaken in chapter 6.

The hypothetical question posed by this book's title is, of course, a metaphorical question that can only be answered metaphorically. In the logic of this book, if God were a human rights activist, for those who believe in Him/Her according to progressive theologies, He or She would definitely be pursuing a counterhegemonic conception of human rights and a practice fully coherent with it. In so doing, this God would sooner or later confront the God invoked by the oppressors, and would find no affinity with this other God. In other words, He or She would come to the conclusion that the God of the subalterns cannot but be a subaltern God. The logical consequence of such a conclusion would be rather illogical from a human point of view, at least as regards the monotheistic religions that have provided the background for my inquiry: a monotheistic God making a plea for polytheism as the only solution, if the invocation of God in social and political struggles for progressive social transformation is not to lead to perverse results. The subaltern God's idea would be that only polytheism allows for an unequivocal answer to the crucial question: Which side are you on? I recognize that a monotheistic God pleading for a polytheistic set of Gods and thus for His or Her own sacrificial suicide for the sake of humankind is an absurd hypothesis. But I wonder if the role of most theologies has not been to prevent us from confronting this absurdity and drawing the conclusions therefrom. As if all along the logos of God had been a human exercise meant to prevent God from speaking Her or His plurality.

Notes

Preface and Acknowledgments

1. The historicity of the opposition between the foundations of human rights and religion is more complex than what this polarization may suggest. With different arguments, Hans Joas (2013) also claims that the antireligious Enlightenment is not the only source of modern human rights and that the preconditions for human rights include the belief in the sacredness of every person and in what such belief entails.

2. Santos, Boaventura de Sousa. 2009. "If God were a Human Rights Activist: Human Rights and the Challenge of Political Theologies," *Law, Social Justice & Global Development* (March 11).

Chapter 1

1. Referring to the global diffusion of human rights discourse as a grammar of social change after the post–Cold War period, Mark Goodale says that "the discursive geography of social change has undergone a seismic shift" (2013: 7).

2. The liberal matrix conceives of human rights as individual rights while privileging civic and political rights. Upon this matrix, other conceptions of human rights evolved, namely those inspired by Marxist or, more generally, socialist ideas that recognize collective rights and privilege economic and social rights over civic and political rights. On the different conceptions of human rights, see Santos (1995: 250–378; 2007c: 3–40).

3. Moyn (2010) considers human rights to be the last utopia, the grand political mission that emerges after the collapse of all the others. His insightful historical analysis on human rights is in some aspects convergent with my own. See also Goodale (2009b).

4. A first formulation of these illusions can be read in Santos (1995: 327–64). Such illusions are a "regimen of truth" being legitimized as a theory that is not subject to denial by human rights practices occurring in its name. This is also Goodale's (2009b) core argument. Goodale convincingly argues how important the anthropological approach to human rights is.

5. This point is also made by Moyn (2010: 89–90), who adds that neither Gandhi nor Sukarno nor Nasser viewed a doctrine of human rights as an empowering instrument.

6. "Napoleon's Proclamation to the Egyptians, 2 July 1798," cited in Hurewitz (1975:

116). Viewed from "The other side of the line," from the side of the invaded, Napoleon's Proclamation fooled no one as to its imperialist objectives. This is how the Egyptian chronicler, Al-Jabarti, an eyewitness of the invasion, dissects the proclamation point by point: "Then [Napoleon] proceeds to something even worse than that, may God cast him into perdition, with his words: 'I more than the Mamluks serve God . . .' There is no doubt that this is a derangement of his mind and an excess of foolishness." Al-Jabarti then exposes the grammatical errors in the weak Qur'anic Arabic of the proclamation and concludes: "However, it is possible that there is no inversion and that the meaning is 'I have more troops or more money than the Mamluks . . .' So his words 'I serve God' are a new sentence and new lie" ([1798] 1993: 31).

7. For a detailed analysis of this issue, see Arendt (1951, 1990).

8. This is what is happening today in many countries of the European Union, countries struck by the economic and financial crisis of the euro zone.

9. Long before Arendt, in 1843 Marx (1977) addressed the same ambiguity between citizenship rights and human rights.

10. The monolithism of the Universal Declaration, even within the borders of the "Western world," is far more apparent than real. Just think of the differences of interpretation made public from the very beginning in the 1948 UNESCO book of commentaries on and interpretations of the Declaration. The remarks by Jacques Maritain, Harold Laski, Teilhard de Chardin, Benedetto Croce, and Salvador Mandariaga about the Declaration are particularly elucidating in this regard. If the Declaration had very little to do with the realities of the "non-Western world," even with regards to the "Western world" the norms established by it were far from being uncontroversial or long-standing truths. Laski's bitter commentary is quite revealing: "It is of the first importance, if a document of this kind is to have lasting influence and significance, to remember that the Great Declarations of the past are a quite special heritage of Western civilization, that they are deeply involved in a Protestant bourgeois tradition, which is itself an outstanding aspect of the rise of the middle class to power, and that, though their expression is universal in its form, the attempts at realization which lie behind that expression have too rarely reached below the level of the middle class. 'Equality before the law' has not meant very much in the lives of the working-class in most political communities, and still less to Negroes in the Southern states of the United States. 'Freedom of Association' was achieved by trade unions in Great Britain only in 1871; in France, save for a brief interval in 1848, only in 1884; in Germany only in the last years of the Bismarckian era, and then but partially; and, in a real way, in the USA only with the National Labor Relations Act of 1935; this Act itself is now in serious jeopardy in Congress. All rights proclaimed in the great documents of this character are in fact statements of aspiration, the fulfillment of which is limited by the view taken by the ruling class of any political community of its relations to the security of interests they are determined to maintain" (1948: 65).

11. Available at http://www.un.org/esa/socdev/unpfii/documents/DRIPS_en.pdf (accessed October 27, 2014).

12. Another dimension of the illusion of monolithism is the issue of the Western cultural premises of human rights and the quest for an intercultural conception of

human rights. This is addressed in this book only with regard to the relationship between human rights and political theologies. I address this dimension more generally elsewhere; see Santos (2007c). See also An-Na'im (1992), Eberhard (2002), Merry (2006), Goodale (2009a).

13. In the sense used here, "conventional" means being less than hegemonic and more than dominant. If we consider the world as a whole as the "relevant audience," the understanding of the human rights presented here is far from being consensually accepted or commonsensical; however, on the other hand, it is not dominant in the sense of being the result of some overriding coercive imposition (even if at times that is the case). For many people in the world it is too entrenched a concept to be possible to fight against and too foreign a concept to be worth fighting for.

14. Another way of addressing the ontological issue is to argue that human rights are neither moral claims nor truth claims. They are political demands and their global appeal does not presuppose any universally accepted moral foundation. This point is forcefully made by Goodhart (2013: 36). The question is why such a global appeal remains unanswered.

Chapter 2

1. Here is my definition of globalization: "the process by which a given local condition or entity succeeds in extending its reach over the globe and, by doing so, develops the capacity to designate a rival social condition or entity as local." The most important implications of this definition are the following. First, in the conditions of the Western capitalist world-system there is no genuine globalization. What we call globalization is always the successful globalization of a given localism. In other words, there is no global condition for which we cannot find a local root, a specific source of cultural embeddedness. Second, globalization entails localization. Thus it would be equally correct in analytical terms if we were to define the current situation and our research topics in terms of localization rather than globalization. The reason we prefer the latter term is basically because hegemonic scientific discourse tends to prefer the story of the world as told by the winners (Santos, 2002a). Available at http://www.eurozine.com/articles/2002-08-22-santos-en.html (accessed on October 27, 2014).

2. The crisis of global financial capital that erupted in the summer of 2008 showed the structural contradictions of the current model of neoliberal globalization. The way the crisis will be "solved" may signal the profile of a new, emergent model.

3. See Keck and Sikkink (1998), Young and Everitt (2004), Garwood (2005), Smith (2005), and Smith and Wiest (2012).

4. The Gramscian concept of hegemony refers to the intellectual stance by a given social class that, however determined by its particular interests, manages to be consensually adopted by other classes. In terms of this conception, counterhegemonic globalization points necessarily to a postcapitalist society, a society in which the ideas of the capitalist classes no longer are consensual beyond class boundaries. In reality, within the movements that fight against neoliberal globalization we can identify two views of hegemony. One, closer to Gramsci, views neoliberal hegemony as a class hegemony to be

fought against through class struggle, in the name of a postcapitalist future. The other views it as a market ideology, hostile to the redistribution of social wealth and income, which is socially accepted as a necessary consequence of freedom and autonomy. The struggle against this hegemony may involve different classes and its objectives may point to postneoliberal futures rather than to postcapitalist futures.

5. On this see a detailed discussion in Joas (2014).

6. On globalized localism and its twin concept of localized globalism, see Santos (2002a). Available at http://www.eurozine.com/articles/2002-08-22-santos-en.html (accessed October 27, 2014).

7. Juan José Tamayo offers one of the most consistent and solid foundations for a liberation theology (1993, 2004a, 2004b). For an overall survey of liberation theology in its forty years, see Leonardo Boff (1973, 1986, 1997). Available at http://leonardoboff .wordpress.com/2011/08/09/quarenta-anos-da-teologia-da-libertacao/ (accessed October 27, 2014). For some examples of Islamic liberation theology, see Asghar Ali Engineer (1990, 1998), Hamid Dabashi (2008), and Arzu Merali and Javad Sharbaf (2009).

8. There are many ways of distinguishing the different models of relationship between religion and sociopolitical and cultural institutions. For instance, Rosemary Ruether, restricting her analysis to Christianity, distinguishes the following models: various kinds of separatism—prophetic, apocalyptic, mystical, or utopian; amalgamation into sacral nations and empires; and various efforts to coexist with and transform society (1991: 218).

9. For a critique of Islamophobia, see, for example, Ramadan (2002), Sayyid (2003), Betz and Meret (2009), as well as Sayyid and Vakil (2010).

10. Douglas Pratt uses the conventional characterizations of Islamic fundamentalism—which he distinguishes from extremism, the latter yielding acts of violence—to analyze different forms of Christian fundamentalism. And he concludes: "Religious fundamentalism issues in multifarious forms of extremism. Islamic extremists may have caught attention and headlines; Christian extremism has somewhat less so. But extremism, as with fundamentalism, is found within all religions . . . Historically, Christianity has known extremism in a number of guises. Often these have involved the application of violence for political and spiritual ends or the engagement in violent clashes in respect to competitive theologies and so on; this is a matter of historical record. Both marginalised and fanatical variants of the faith have arisen and have themselves been the subject of repressive and extreme measures. In the contemporary world there is evidence of an upsurge in fundamentalist mentality and groupings within Christianity sufficient to suggest that fundamentalist extremism is not just the province of Islam but that Christianity is able to produce similar extreme ideology and related actions. Christianity knows its own extremities and its fanatics; fundamentalism can and does yield extremism; extremism can and has yielded terroristic violence" (2010: 454).

11. For the history of the term and typologies of fundamentalist features, see Emerson and Hartman (2006: 127–44). In part as a result of the rise of theological fundamentalism in our time, the term "fundamentalism" has been increasingly used beyond its religious context as a metaphor to characterize behaviors or attitudes based on ir-

reducible beliefs in such fields as political activism, identity politics, or nationalism. See Nagata (2001).

12. *American Mercury,* October (1925: 158–60).

13. To go deeper into the topic of Christian fundamentalism, see, for instance, the works of Juan José Tamayo (2004a, 2004b), George Marsden (2006), Anselmo Borges (2010: 74–86), José Casanova (1994: 135–66), and David New (2012). Further below I deal with the current versions of this Christian fundamentalism as it reemerged in the United States in the 1980s associated with the New Christian Right.

14. See also Tamayo (2009).

15. For an overall panorama of the discussion of the place of historical reason in the interpretation of Christian revelation, see Queiruga (1987). For different perspectives on this topic in Islamic contexts, see, for example, Al-Azmeh and János M. Bak (2004), Özsoy (2006), Tibi (2005), and Ramadan (2002).

16. According to the Free Dictionary, "integrism" (French: intégrisme) is a term coined in early twentieth-century polemics within the Catholic Church, especially in France, as an epithet to describe those who opposed the "modernists," who sought to create a synthesis between Christian theology and the liberal philosophy of secular modernity. The term was originally used by dissidents during the time of Pope St. Pius X, whose papacy was between 1903 and 1914, in attacks on Catholics who upheld his encyclicals such as Pascendi Dominici Gregis and most significantly Pius IX's Syllabus of Errors, which specifically condemned the modernist position. Those who were called "integrists," or regarded themselves as defenders of Sacred Tradition, contrary to the modernists sought the continuation of traditional Catholic truths, which they claim, have always been taught. Some critics have framed this within a sociopolitical context of a general opposition to the secular modernity of the Western world. As represented chiefly by the revolution in France of 1789 and the ascent in society of a secular bourgeoise leadership caste, who were often cosmopolitan, republican, and anticlerical in worldview. By the late twentieth century, these elements were strong critics of the "spirit of Vatican II," emerging from the Second Vatican Council, including the suppression of the Tridentine Rite and some of the Council itself. The term "integrism" is largely restricted to French sociopolital parlance, while the term "traditional Catholics" has become more prominent in recent times and is generally the most common term used in the Anglosphere to describe antimodernist elements. The term has also been borrowed in some cultures to describe elements within non-Catholic religious movements who are also opposed to the radical end of Western liberalism, such as Protestant fundamentalism or Islamism. Available at http://www.thefreedictionary.com/integrism (accessed October 27, 2014). On the distinction between Protestant or Islamic fundamentalism and Catholic integrism, see Lathuilière (1995).

17. For an alternative way of "reclaiming the caliphate," see the pathbreaking work of Sayyid (2014).

18. Barzilai-Nahon and Barzilai analyze the relationship between the Internet and religious fundamentalism based on an empirical examination of ultraorthodox Jewish communities in Israel. They propose the concept of "cultured technology" as "a means to

understand how the Internet has been culturally constructed, modified, and adapted to the needs of fundamentalist communities, and how they in turn have been affected by it" (2005: 25).

19. On the history of traditionalism as related to Christian theology, see Metz (1980: 20–22).

20. Available at http://www.servicioskoinonia.org/relat/229.htm (accessed October 27, 2014). For works providing a survey of liberation theologies, see note 7 above in this chapter, and notes 1 and 7 in chapter 6.

21. See also Tamayo (2011).

22. Tamayo's and Fornet-Betancourt's intercultural theology distinguishes itself from Hans Küng's *weltethos* project. According to Küng, "there will be no peace among nations without peace among religions. There will be no peace among religions without dialogue among religions. There will be no dialogue among religions without global ethical standards. There will therefore be no survival of this globe without a global ethic." Available at http://www.peaceproposal.com/Kung.html (accessed on October 27, 2014). This conception dismisses the importance of diversity and the historical, political, and economic conditions that made it the way it is today. See Tariq Ramadan's (2005a) response to Hans Küng.

23. As Moltmann says: "The product of organized religion is an institutionalized absence of commitment. Faith becomes a private affair, and the articles of the creed can be replaced at will. This, then, is a religion that demands nothing; so it ceases to console anyone either . . . This is the justification of what exists, but without judgment" (1982: 159).

24. See, among others, Fiorenza (1994), Theissen and Merz (1998), and Crossan (1991).

25. On other postcolonial theologies, see Felix Wilfred (2000, 2002, 2009); R. S. Sugirtharajah (2002, 2005); Catherine Keller, Michael Nausner, and Mayra Rivera (2004); Namsoon Kang (2004); Mark Lewis Taylor (2004); Mayra Rivera (2007); and Musa Dube, Andrew Mbuvi, and Dora Mbuwayesango (2012). For a feminist postcolonial perspective, see also Kwok Pui-lan (2005).

26. For feminist Christian theologies, see Teresa Toldy (2011, 2012); Elisabeth Schüssler Fiorenza (1984, 1992, 1993, 1998, 2011); Mary Daly (1968, 1973); Sally McFague (2000, 2008); Rosemary Radford Ruether (1993, 2011); Carol Christ (1998, 2004); Marcella Althaus-Reid and Lisa Isherwood (2007); Ivone Gebara (1998); Ada María Isasi-Díaz and Yolanda Tarango (1988); Virginia Fabella and Mercy Amba Oduyoye (1988); María Pilar Aquino (1996); and Ursula King (1994). For feminist Islamic theologies, see Leila Ahmed (1992), Asma Barlas (2006), Shahrzad Mojab (2001), Amina Wadud (1999, 2006), Heba Raouf Ezzat (2001), and Margot Badran (2009).

27. See more on this in chapter 6.

Chapter 3

1. Under Western colonialism, many non-Western and non-Christian religions were the object of Christian-based theological reflection, which, in general, reproduced the Western colonialist prejudices about the "other." An illustration of this is the ori-

entalist conception of Islamic theology of Duncan MacDonald (1903). For a critique, see Moosa (2005: 14). For a very profound analysis (even if saturated with a Western Enlightenment conception of rationalism), see the monumental work of Josef van Ess (1991–1997, 2006) on the Islamic theology of the classical period, the second and third centuries of Hidschra. On orientalism and "orientalism in reverse" concerning the study of Islam in France, see the polemical analysis by Achcar (2007).

2. The relationship between political Islam and Western modernity is analyzed by Roy (1994), who also raises the problems of comparativism in this area: "Why does Western Orientalism study Islam *sub specie aeternitatis*, while approaching Western civilization as a 'socio-historical configuration'?" (1994: 11)

3. If such general evaluations were warranted, I would consider Christian Zionism the most dangerous of all, given its role in the nonsolution of the Israel-Palestine conflict. See Ateek, Duaybis, and Tobin (2005).

4. The cautionary note on the internal diversity of Islam is even more necessary as the Western media tend to portray it as a monolithic religion. An overview of such diversity can be read in Donohue and Esposito (1982). As is the case with Christianity, there is in Islam an immense variety of political theologies both with regards to their range and to their criteria for intervention in society. Gilbert Achcar disputes this equation between Christianity and Islam. In a comparative Marxist analysis of Christian theologies of liberation and Islamic fundamentalism—or Orthodox Islam, as he also calls it—Achcar (2008) contrasts the "elective affinity" between Orthodox Islam and Medieval-reactionary utopianism with the "elective affinity" between original Christianity and the communistic utopianism from which liberation theology draws its inspiration. The problem with this comparison is that liberation theologies are pluralist theologies rather than fundamentalist ones. If the comparison were between Islamic fundamentalism and Christian fundamentalism, today on the rise, we would easily see two "combative ideologies contesting the prevailing social and/or political conditions" (2008: 56), both backward looking and thus equally reactionary.

5. An exhaustive bibliographical account of the Western academic perspective on Islam, Muslims, and Islamic countries in the last decades can be read in the multivolume work of Saied Reza Ameli (2012).

6. As an illustration, see for the case of Mozambique, where the number of faithfuls to Islam is on the rise (Bonate, 2006, 2007a, 2007b). See more generally as well Eickelman and Piscatori (2004).

7. For a brief survey of the diversity of *shari'a* interpretations, see, for instance, Hallaq (2004) or Fletcher (2006). The Sufi hermeneutics of *shari'a* must also be taken into account, according to which "the ongoing challenges of each age must be met anew with spiritual resources and responses suitable to current needs" (Ernst, 2006: 5). This impacts on the possibility of bringing interpretations of *shari'a* up to date. The story goes that in the sixteenth century Muhammad Chishti commented on the spiritual practice of the Chishti masters of listening to music like this: "It is related of the revered Shaykh Hasan Muhammad that a man of Lahore came and said, 'In this time there is no one worthy of listening to music' [sama]. [The master] replied, 'if there were no one

worthy of listening to music, the world would be destroyed.' The man said, 'In times past, there were men like Shaykh Nasir ad-Din [Chiragh-I Dihli], the Emperor of the Shaykhs [Nizam ad-Din Awliya], and the revered [Farid ad-Din] Ganj-i Shakkar. Now there is no one like them.' [The master] answered, 'In their time, men said the very same thing'" (Ernst, 2006: 5).

8. For a different view of the Muslim Brotherhood, see Roy (1994). Achcar also draws our attention to the need to distinguish between varying and contrasting brands of Islamic fundamentalism: "Thus there is a huge difference, for instance, between, on the one hand, an organization like the most reactionary al-Qaeda, which is waging in Iraq a bloody war of sectarian extermination along with its fight against US occupation, and holds a truly totalitarian conception of society and polity; and, on the other hand, a movement such as Lebanese Hezbollah which condemns 'political sectarianism' in the name of its fight against Israeli occupation and aggression and, even while considering the 'Islamic Republic' of Iran as its supreme earthly model, acknowledges the religious plurality of Lebanon and consequently upholds the principles of parliamentary democracy" (2008: 73).

9. See also Hussein Solomon (2005). Oliver Roy distinguishes between political Islam or Islamism and neofundamentalism, tracing their differences on three major issues: state power, *shari'a*, and women (1994: 34–47). According to him, while Islamism aims at revolutionary state power (illustrated by the case of Iran), neofundamentalism privileges a bottom-up, society-based transformation. For a radical critique of Roy and the erratic evolution of his analysis of Islam, see Achcar (2007). Commenting on the political manipulation of the topic "political Islam," Casanova argues: "Every incrimination of Islam as a fundamentalist, anti-modern and anti-Western religion could have been directed even more justifiably against Catholicism not long ago. Moreover, most features of contemporary political Islam which Western observers find rightly so reprehensible, including the terrorist methods and the justification of revolutionary violence as an appropriate instrument in the pursuit of political power, can be found in the not too distant past of many Western countries and of many modern secular movements. Thus, before attributing these reprehensible phenomena all too hastily to Islamic civilization one should perhaps consider the possibility that global modernity itself somehow generates such practices" (2011: 261).

10. For an early view of the shift from nationalism to "revolutionary Islam," see Arjomand (1984). A different analysis can be found in Achcar (2008).

11. Salman Sayyd forcefully argues against the Western-centric commonsensical conception of secularism as a necessary stage or condition of world peaceful development rather than as a contingent product of European history: "The case for secularism as necessary for civic peace is largely based on extrapolating instances/narratives from the European experiences of the wars of the Reformation and counter-reformation to make a general point about the relationship between civic peace and depoliticisation of religious belief" (2014: 36). Moreover, "is it also the case that the instances of large-scale violence (wars, 'terrorism,' occupation, and riots) are exclusive to religions? Could we not draw up another list in which the starring roles in the perpetuation of great cruelty and violence would be ascribed to secularist actors? (2014: 32).

12. The transnationalism of believers (*umma*) is also to be observed in Catholicism, as Casanova (2005) reminds us.

13. See note 8 and consider the distinction between two contrasting conceptions of Islamic fundamentalism: al-Qaeda and Hezbollah.

14. On the WSF, see Santos (2006b).

15. The secular nature of the WSF refers to the principle of the separation of state and religion. But, in light of the Charter of Principles, it cannot be said to be secularist (the reduction of pluralism in the public sphere to nonreligious stances), since faith-based progressive movements have been part of it since the beginning. In apparent contradiction with this, however, two situations must be addressed critically. First, since the events of 9/11, Islamic movements and organizations have been the victims of a politics of suspicion deeply entrenched in the orientalist view of Islam as a monolithic entity. This has happened in the organization of some regional meetings of the WSF and must be denounced vigorously. Second, in some areas of social struggle, such as feminism, secularist conceptions are by far paramount, and the dominant movements and discourses may at times exclude religious feminist perspectives, particularly in the case of Islam. For a very thoughtful critical analysis of the secularism of the WSF that was held in Mumbai in 2004, see Daulatzai (2004).

16. Throughout this book, I emphasize that, in the case of Islam, as well as in the case of all the other major religions, the opposition to counterhegemonic globalization is restricted to the conceptions and practices expounded by the fundamentalist political theologies. Unfortunately, in the case of Islam, this restriction has not always been borne in mind by organizers or supporters of counterhegemonic struggles. Suffice it to mention the controversy that surrounded the participation of Tariq Ramadan in the European Social Forum of 2003. Ramadan (2004) is one of the Islamic intellectuals who have most forcefully argued for the congruence between Islam and progressive, counterhegemonic struggles while criticizing the dominant protagonists of such struggles for a lack of openness to the world of Islam . One of the most disgraceful dimensions of the controversy was the accusation of anti-Semitism against Ramadan. See Mannot and Ternisien (2003).

17. Manneke Budiman (2008: 73) reports that, in post-Suharto Indonesia, and facing radicalizing Islamic tendencies, "women's movements . . . have to remake the image of feminism in Indonesian terms so that it cannot be dismissed as an ideology imported from the West and, simultaneously, they must develop a home-grown counter-discourse against the mainstream interpretation of sacred texts by using the same sources of knowledge that the Islamists employ." This is not the place to analyze the alleged "elective affinities" between Western modernity, especially in its liberal version (primacy of law and individual rights), and women's liberation, or, conversely, to assess the patriarchal nature of capitalism and the intrinsic limits of the struggles against sexual discrimination in capitalist societies. For a good overall view of these themes, see Weisberg (1993).

18. I address this position and its potential for an intercultural dialogue with human rights in Santos (2007c). Some authors suggest that there are possible articulations be-

tween Islamic feminism and liberation theology (Tohidi, 1997; Mojab, 2001). The debate on Islamic feminism is immense. See, among others, Mernissi (1987, 1991, 1996), Ahmed (1992), Yamani (1996), Karam (1998), Afsaruddin (1999), Mojab (2001), Abbas-Gholiza-deh (2001), Ezzat (2001), Shahidian (2002), Moghadam (2002), Barlas (2002), Gresh (2004), Shaik (2004), Ramadan (2005b), Ziba Mir-Hosseini (2006), Wadud (2006), Edwin (2006), and Badran (2009).

19. See, for instance, Mir-Hosseini (1996, 2006), Ebadi (2006), Budiman (2008), and Salime (2011).

20. For an overall survey of the xenophobic and Islamophobic manipulation of discourses on Islamic women's rights, see, for example, Mohanty (1991), Okin (1999), Spivak (2002), Razack (2004, 2007), Al-Ali (2005), Skenderovic (2006), Coene and Long-man (2010), and Toldy (2011, 2012).

Chapter 4

1. But Catholic fundamentalism (commonly designated as integrism; see note 16 in chapter 2) has always been present, particularly in Europe and Latin America, taking different forms and degrees of radicalness: Opus Dei, Engelswerk, Spanish integrism, Lefebvrism (inspired by bishop Marcel Lefebvre). As we shall see, there are also streaks of fundamentalism among prominent theologians of the Roman Catholic Church.

2. One can find a good analysis of Falwell's pressure group politics in Bruce (1990).

3. Available at http://www.garynorth.com/freebooks/whatsice.htm (accessed October 27, 2014).

4. North is considered one of the representatives of so-called "dominion theology." According to Theocracy Watch (2005), open advocates of dominionism declare that "America is a Christian Nation," and that therefore Christians have a God-given mandate to reassert Christian control over political, social, and cultural institutions. Yet many dominionists stop short of staking out a position that could be called theocratic. This is the "soft" version of dominionism. The "hard" version is explicitly theocratic or "theonomic," as the Christian Reconstructionists prefer to be called. Available at http://www.theocracywatch.org/dominionism.htm (accessed October 27, 2014).

5. In its popular version, this gospel was introduced by well-known church ministers from the USA. For instance, A. A. Allen became one of the first ministers to appeal to fundraising, by teaching that God is a rich God, and that those who want to share in his prosperity must obey and support God's servant—the speaker himself (Akoko, 2007: 67). The involvement of churches in business ventures as a way of raising income for their activities is justified by the idea that the gospel message is meant for the poor and frustrated, the socially excluded. The fact that social inequality and exclusion have been intensified by the neoliberal capitalist policies these theologies subscribe to is conspicuously omitted. In Africa, for example, the adoption of World Bank/IMF structural adjustment policies in the mid and late 1980s fuelled the quest for spiritual and religious solutions to people's many problems.

6. The prosperity message is broad and goes much beyond economic and material prosperity; it also involves prosperity in body, soul, and spirit, which has to do with issues such as healing ability, peace, protection, and deliverance, among others. On this topic, see Brouwer and Rose (1996), Coleman (2000), Corten and Marshall-Fratani (2001), and Brown (2011).

7. "Speech delivered before the Mont Pelerin Society in Sri Lanka on January 11, 2004." Available at http://www.nationalreview.com/articles/209555/wealth-virtue (accessed October 27, 2014). For a reading that is, if not laudatory, at least acritical of capitalism, which tends to replace state-coordinated social justice with charity and philanthropy, see Leite (2012) on the current trend maintained by some top CEOs in European countries hit by the crisis, in which the "criterion of enterprising administration" is love.

8. Confronted with massive protests, Marco Feliciano was forced to resign and the proposed law was withdrawn from the parliament's agenda.

9. See "Africa: How the American Christian Right Has Promoted African Anti-Gay Laws," available at http://www.dailymaverick.co.za/article/2014-01-20-the-bigger-picture-understanding-anti-gay-laws-in-africa/#.U5j3ZSguJVI (accessed October 27, 2014).

10. This bill is available at http://wp.patheos.com.s3.amazonaws.com/blogs/warrenthrockmorton/files/2014/02/Anti-Homosexuality-Act-2014.pdf (accessed October 27, 2014).

11. The bill is available at http://www.placng.org/new/laws/Same%20Sex%20Marriage%20%28Prohibition%29%20Act,%202013.pdf (accessed October 27, 2014).

12. Available at http://www.news24.com/Africa/News/1st-Uganda-gay-sex-trial-since-tough-new-law-20140508 (accessed October 27, 2014).

13. "Catholic bishops oppose gays Bill," available at http://www.monitor.co.ug/News/National/-/688334/840276/-/wh9b6q/-/index.html (accessed October 27, 2014).

14. See "The Religious Right in East Africa: Slain by the Spirit," available at http://www.economist.com/node/16488830 (accessed October 27, 2014); "It's Not Just Uganda: Behind the Christian Right's Onslaught in Africa," available at http://www.thenation.com/blog/179191/its-not-just-uganda-behind-christian-rights-onslaught-africa# (accessed October 27, 2014); and "The Bait of Christian Fundamentalism in Africa," available at http://www.huffingtonpost.com/michael-mungai/christian-fundamentalism-africa_b_935268.html (accessed October 27, 2014).

15. As noted above, Islamic fundamentalism, also on the rise in Africa, coincides with Christian fundamentalism in criminalizing sexual minorities and, more generally, in denying reproductive and sexual orientation rights.

16. The support granted Republican candidates by Protestant conservatives continues. See the data about the 2012 presidential elections provided by The Pew Forum on Religion & Public Life: "At the other end of the political spectrum, nearly eight-in-ten white evangelical Protestants voted for Romney (79%), compared with 20% who backed Obama. Romney received as much support from evangelical voters as George W. Bush did in 2004 (79%) and more support from evangelicals than McCain did in 2008

(73%). Mormon voters were also firmly in Romney's corner; nearly eight-in-ten Mormons (78%) voted for Romney, while 21% voted for Obama. Romney received about the same amount of support from Mormons that Bush received in 2004. (Exit poll data on Mormons was unavailable for 2000 and 2008.)" Available at http://www.pewforum.org/Politics-and-Elections/How-the-Faithful-Voted-2012-Preliminary-Exit-Poll-Analysis.aspx#rr (accessed October 27, 2014). In Western Europe, the links between Catholic fundamentalism and extreme right politics have also been analyzed. See, for the case of Austria, Told (2004), Camus (2007), and Rosenberger and Hadj-Abdou (2013).

17. "What's the difference between BNP and Ukip voters?" available at http://www.theguardian.com/commentisfree/2014/apr/14/bnp-ukip-voters-politics-immigration (accessed October 27, 2014).

18. The same is, of course, true of Jewish fundamentalism, as most forcefully argued by Yuval-Davis (1992), a founder member of the Women Against Fundamentalism.

19. I am aware of Sayyid's critique of this approach. For Sayyid, Sahgal and Yuval-Davis's "concept of fundamentalism relies not on its internal coherence but, rather, on a 'shared' assumption regarding the role of politics, truth and religion. My criticism of [the concept of] fundamentalism is based on the impossibility of using it as the ground upon which to carry out a meaningful comparison between, for example, the BJP, Likud, the Muslim Brotherhood, the Christian Coalition, and so on" (2003: 15–16).

20. For more information on this topic, see, for example, Bayes and Tohidi (2001) and Madigan (2010).

21. See "Código penal moçambicano viola direitos humanos das mulheres e crianças [Mozambican penal code violates human rights of women and children]. Available at http://pt.globalvoicesonline.org/2014/03/19/codigo-penal-mocambicano-viola-direitos-humanos-das-mulheres-e-criancas/ (accessed October 27, 2014) and "The Power of Civil Society: A Concrete Mozambican Example," available at http://www.dailymaverick.co.za/article/2014-04-09-the-power-of-civil-society-a-concrete-mozambican-example/#.U5yufCguJVI (accessed October 27, 2014).

Chapter 5

1. I deal with Western monocultures and their alternatives in detail in Santos (2004, 2014).

2. The complexity of relations between Islam and Western modernity is well illustrated by Ebrahim Moosa when he writes: "Like the well-intentioned labours of Muslim modernists a century ago, progressive Muslims run the risk of becoming servants of power. The state-driven modernizing of Islam has turned Muslim modernists into partners and servants of the most brutal authoritarian regimes from Egypt to Pakistan and from Tunisia to Indonesia. Muslim progressives might have to consider the value of entering the democratic base of their societies rather than placating elites" (2006: 127).

3. In Santos (2007c), I propose an intercultural translation between human rights principles and non-Western principles of human dignity.

4. I analyze the binary roots/options in greater detail in Santos (1998).

5. See also Almond, Appleby, and Sivan (2003).

6. On this issue, see Santos (2007a).

7. For different perspectives on the roots of Arab nationalism, see, for instance, Hopwood (1999).

8. See, among others, Fischer (1980) and Dabashi (1993).

9. Secularity is a philosophical and political stance that defends the separation of state and religion but admits the presence of nonsecular stances in the public sphere, whereas secularism is the embodiment of the public sphere itself as the sole authoritative source of public reason, thus leaving no room for nonsecular stances in the public space.

10. This is forcefully argued by Nandy (1985, 1998), although I do not share the consequences he draws from his argument. In my view, as in the case of human rights and globalization, there is room for a decolonizing, counterhegemonic, radically democratic secularity. For the defenders of secularism, who refuse to distinguish the latter from secularity (see note 9 above), such radically democratic secularity will be a disguised postsecularism. To discuss this in detail is beyond the scope of this book. The religious positions vis-à-vis secularism are both theologically and politically motivated. Above all, they are contextual, both in historical and sociological terms. For instance, Muslims in India, feeling threatened by the rise of Hindu extremism, tend to have a nuanced view of secularism. According to Mushir Ul-Haq: "If secularism places worldly life outside the control of religion, this is an innovation without precedent in Islamic history; hence, it is unacceptable for the faithful. But if secularism denotes only that the state does not favour any particular community in matters of religion, it is believed to be in accord with Islamic tradition which gives religious freedom to every citizen. This concept of secularism is not alien to a Muslim and therefore he sees no conflict between his religion, Islam and secularism" (1982: 177).

11. See Toldy (2007) on the different conceptions of secularization and secularism. See also Robin Archer: "Even if we look only at one small subset of Western societies—those rooted in English cultural, political and economic traditions—we find a full range of possible outcomes. The United States has a secular state, but not a secularized society. Britain has a secularized society, but not a secular state. And only Australia has both a secular state and a secularized society. Moreover, even where similar outcomes have been achieved in different Western societies, these outcomes have often been reached by very different paths. Both the United States and France have established secular states. But in France this was achieved by mobilizing militant antireligious movements, while in the United States it was achieved without any such mobilization. Likewise, both Britain and France have largely secularized societies. But in France secularization was accompanied by massive conflicts between church and state, while in Britain such conflicts were limited" (2001: 204; see also Casanova, 1994). In the past decade, the most innovative analyses of secularism have come from the global South. See, for instance, Bhargava (1998), with a specific focus on India. But see also Connolly (1999) and, most recently, the monumental treatise of Charles Taylor (2007).

12. One other issue I do not treat here is the current debate in the West concerning the future of secularism. In recent years, several authors have taken issue with secular-

ism for its incapacity to account for the "plurivocity of being," to use William Connolly's phrase (1999), that is to say, for preventing beliefs other than the secularist belief from expressing themselves in the public sphere. See also Taylor (2007). For a specific focus on law, see Fitzpatrick (2007). Whether explicitly recognized or not, this debate is being fueled by the increasing visibility of "the other" inside the West. See Asad (2003).

13. Elisabeth Schüssler Fiorenza, for instance, calls attention to the production of a religious ideology based on structural male domination—political, racial, and class domination that translates itself into global oppression, in other words, into a kyrio-centric system, a pyramid of multiple oppressions (1992: 114–32). In her view, patriarchy is not a binary sexual system, but rather a complex pyramidal structure of political dom-ination and subordination, stratified according to taxonomies of sex, race, class, religion, and culture. Religion is an important piece of the "kyriarchical discourse" (1994: 100).

14. To be more precise, there is no single historical process of secularization; there are several, even inside Europe where this process is said to be at home. In this respect, see the work of Joas (2014), in which the author shows cogently how contingent the relation between modernization and secularization is.

15. On cognitive injustice see Santos (2007b, 2014).

16. On subaltern cosmopolitanism, see Santos (2002b: 465–70).

17. In 2004 in Iraq a telling example was the way in which the violations of prison-ers' human rights in the prison of Abu Ghraib were trumpeted worldwide in order to further occult a more massive violation of human rights: the invasion and occupation of Iraq.

18. The emphasis on duties is not in itself an obstacle to intercultural translation and an ecology of knowledges with human rights. Such an obstacle exists only when the duties are conceived of as emanating from a transcendental, humanly uncontrol-lable and unintelligible command. This-world–based conceptions of the primacy of duties may indeed be a motive for fruitful dialogues with human rights discourses and practices. A famous formulation of this type of conception is Mahatma Gandhi's let-ter addressed to the Director-General of UNESCO on May 25, 1947: "I learnt from my illiterate but wise mother that all rights to be deserved and preserved came from duty well done. Thus the very right to live accrues to us only when we do the duty of citizenship of the world. From this one fundamental statement, perhaps it is easy enough to define the duties of Man and Woman and correlate every right to some cor-responding duty to be first performed. Every other right can be shown to be usurpation hardly worth fighting for" (UNESCO, 1948: 3). Available at http://unesdoc.unesco.org/images/0015/001550/155042eb.pdf (accessed October 27, 2014).

19. See Moosa: "God is the one who confers rights on persons, via revealed author-ity although human authority mediates these rights" (2004: 6). In this spirit of the pos-sible compatibility of human rights with Islam, An-Na'im writes: "it is better to seek to transform the understanding of Muslims of those aspects of Shari'a, than to confront them with a stark choice between Islam and human rights. Such a choice is not only an offensive violation of freedom of religion or belief, but will also certainly result in the rejection of the human rights paradigm itself by most Muslims" (2006: 791).

20. Tamayo (2003) alludes to a thread running through the Bible, Christianity, and theology suggesting that the relation between God and the human being is only meaningful when liberation and human dignity meet.

21. For an analysis of these constitutional innovations and for the political processes that led to them, see Santos (2010).

Chapter 6

1. The bibliography on Latin American liberation theologies is immense. In my view, Gutiérrez (1971, 2004) and Boff (1973, 1986, 1997) represent the most eloquent formulations of the first generation of liberation theology. The latter illustrates better than anyone else the capacity of liberation theologians to include new issues of social justice, for instance, the liberation of indigenous peoples and of women and, more recently, the ecological issues and the question of a new environmental ethics (1997). An excellent Marxist analysis of Latin American liberation theologies can be found in Löwy (1996). See also the important work by Tamayo (1993, 2004a, 2004b) and note 20 in chapter 2.

2. In order to capture the diversity of approaches that fit under the name of feminist theology I refer the reader, beyond the work of Soelle (1974, 2006), to Loades (1990), King (1994), Kumari (1999), Women's Theologians Fellowship (2002), Aquino (1988), Vuola (2002), Tamez and O'Connell (2006), Ströher (2009), and Toldy (2011, 2012). For intercultural feminist theologies, see Aquino and Rosado-Nunes (2007).

3. On this matter, Elisabeth Schüssler Fiorenza's work is an insurmountable reference. Just by way of example, see Fiorenza (1993).

4. On the issue of violence against women, see, for example, Bergesch (2006). For a queer approach, see, among others, Althaus-Reid and Isherwood (2007).

5. Based on the same broad conception of feminist liberation theology, Welch (2000) develops a "feminist ethic of risk."

6. Starting with the seminal work of Virgilio Elizondo (1975), there is also a Hispanic/Latino theology focusing on the social struggles of Hispanic/Latino people living in the United States. See Valentin (2002) for a convincing plea to move beyond identity politics and address the broader issues of political economy, classism, and racism, a move toward what he designates as "public theology." In this regard it is also important to have in mind the specific traits of an Islamic liberation theology as formulated by Engineer (1990).

7. On black theology, see, among many others, Evans (1987) and Kunnie (1994). For some currents of black liberation theology, see "Jesus is black" Cone (1969); on the other hand, African theologies of inculturation in sub-Saharan Africa usually refer to Jesus as "our brother" or "our Great Ancestor" (Schreiter, 1991). With a specific focus on the Caribbean, see, for instance, Erskine (1998) and Gonzalez (2006). Caribbean perspectives on liberation theology put a specific emphasis on colonialism, which is still very present in institutions and social practices, as well as in everyday life and our own minds. Hence the conceptions of "decolonizing theology" or "theology of decolonization" (Erskine, 1998). Nelson Maldonado-Torres (2006) cautions us against conflating

the "colonial difference" with the "theological difference" and defends the priority of an epistemological decolonizing politics in the construction of a true liberation theology. See also the important work by Lewis Gordon (1995a, 1995b, 2007).

8. For a survey of Palestinian liberation theology, see Robson (2010). On Palestinian initiatives and institutions of dialogue and ecumenical action in this perspective, see Al'Liqa' Center for Religious & Heritage Studies in the Holy Land, available at http://www.al-liqacenter.org.ps/eng/p_materials/Identity.php (accessed October 27, 2014), and International Center of Bethlehem dar annadwa addawliyya, available at (accessed October 27, 2014), as well as Sabeel Ecumenical Liberation Theology Center, available at http://www.sabeel.org/ (accessed October 27, 2014).

9. Gottwald's (1979) masterful work on the history of early, premonarchical Israel, and specifically on the ways the Israelite community settled in Canaan, offers a vivid historical analysis of the coexistence among different peoples in Palestine. Upon this long history a common Jewish and Palestinian liberation theology might be developed.

10. For a Jesuit perspective on liberation theology in Asia, see Arokiasamy and Gispert-Sauch (1987).

11. For an overview of different liberation theologies in different regions of the world, see Tamayo (1993).

12. The same is true of the body as a source of joy through the ideals of pleasure and beauty, which domesticated visceral reactions and potentially explosive experiences. Far from producing inert bodies, the moral codes were founded on them.

13. Theologians of different denominations and orientations have been questioning why age-old religious diversity is today being experienced in novel "new age" ways, giving rise to a new kind of theological reflection, the "theology of religious pluralism" (Hick and Knitter, 1987: 7; see also, Dupuis, 1997, and Knitter, 2002).

14. As happens in general with great religious leaders, Ghazali is a controversial figure and some make him responsible for the reduction of pluralism inside Islam.

15. The contraposition with "historical reconstruction" should not be overstressed, having in mind Koselleck's conceptual and semantic history: "The conditions of possibility of real history are, at the same time, conditions of its cognition. Hope and memory, or expressed more generally, expectation and experience—for expectation comprehends more than hope, and experience goes deeper than memory— simultaneously constitute history and its cognition. They do so by demonstrating and producing the inner relation between past and future or yesterday, today, or tomorrow" (2004: 258).

16. The same argument is made by Asad (1993: 63).

17. I follow Panikkar for whom, "spirituality [is] a set of basic attitudes prior to their manifestation in theories, or their unfolding in praxis" (1988: 91).

18. Panikkar describes the early Christians in this way: "They were not living exclusively in history. Eschatology was an ever-present factor. They could fearlessly face death. They were martyrs, witnesses to an event. Fidelity was paramount. This conviction was dominant roughly until the fall of Rome under Alaric in 410, or the death of St. Augustine in 430. The true Christian was a martyr" (1988: 93).

19. Besides martyrdom there are many other forms of spirituality. In Christian theology, for instance, Thanzauva identifies the following additional types of spirituality: monastic, ecclesiastical, reformation, pietistic, evangelical, ecumenical, liberation, feminist, dialogical, indigenous/tribal, communitarian, doxological, and praxiological (2002: 249–72). In Islamic theology, the Sufi tradition attributes a particularly central role to spirituality. See Green (2004), Safi (2005), and Le Gall (2010).

20. Is the suffering God a subaltern God? Is the God of the oppressors the same as the God of the oppressed? Have not the Gods of the colonized populations been despised and suppressed as magic and idolatrous practices by the God of colonial Christianity? Can the suffering God be the God of the whole of Christianity without contradicting Himself or Herself?

21. Such possessive individualism is very different from the one theorized and criticized by Macpherson (1962) and by K. Polanyi (1944) and M. Polanyi (1962). The religious version calls for the withdrawal from the world, while the secular version invites unmediated immersion in economic, social, and political life. But both share a reference to some absolute, transcendental entity that gives meaning to their life options and thus holds together their solitude. In the religious case, it is the unmediated intimacy with a transcendental God or impersonal divinity; in the secular case, it is the unconditional belief in the absolute reliability of the capitalist markets in guiding their actions.

22. See, for instance, Reza Shah-Kazemi (2006), who compares the "paths to transcendence" of three great mystics in three major religions: Shankara in Hinduism, Ibn Arabi in Islam, and Meister Eckhart in Christianity.

References

Abbas-Gholizadeh, Mahboubeh. 2001. "The Experience of Islamic Feminism in Iran." Special issue on Reform and the Women's Movement, *Farzaneh* 5(10), 3–6.

Achcar, Gilbert. 2006. *The Clash of Barbarisms: The Making of the New World Disorder.* Boulder, CO: Paradigm.

———. 2007. "Orientalism in Reverse: Post-1979 Trends in French Orientalism." Fourth Annual Edward Said Memorial Lecture at the University of Warwick, November 20.

———. 2008. "Religion and Politics Today from a Marxian Perspective." In *Socialist Register.* Ed. Leo Panitch and Colin Leys. Monmouth, Wales: Merlin, 55–76.

Adichie, Chimamanda. 2014. "Why Can't He Just Be Like Everyone Else?" *Scoop,* Feb. 18. Available at *http://www.thescoopng.com/chimamanda-adichie-why-cant-he-just-be-like-everyone-else/* (accessed October 27, 2014).

Adorno, Theodor. 1955. *Prismen.* Munich: Suhrkamp.

Afsaruddin, Asma, ed. 1999. *Hermeneutics and Honor: Negotiating Female "Public" Space in Islamic/ate Societies.* Cambridge, MA: Harvard University Press.

Ahmed, Leila. 1992. *Women and Gender in Islam: Historical Roots of a Modern Debate.* New Haven, CT: Yale University Press.

Akoko, Robert B. 2007. *"Ask and You Shall Be Given": Pentecostalism and the Economic Crisis in Cameroon.* Leiden, Holland: African Studies Centre.

Al-Ali, Nadje. 2005. "Reconstructing Gender: Iraqi Women between Dictatorship, War, Sanctions and Occupation." *Third World Quarterly* 26(4–5), 739–58.

Al-Azmeh, Aziz, and János M. Bak, eds. 2004. *Monotheistic Kingship: The Medieval Variants.* Series: CEU Medievalia. Budapest: Department of Medieval Studies, Pasts Incorporated, CEU Studies in the Humanities and Central European University Press.

Al-Jabarti, Abd Al-Rahman. [1798] 1993. *Napoleon in Egypt: Al-Jabarti's Chronicle of the French Occupation, 1798.* Trans. Shmuel Moreh. Princeton, NJ: Markus Wiener.

Almond, Gabriel, Scott Appleby, and Emmanuel Sivan. 2003. *Strong Religion: The Rise of Fundamentalisms around the World.* Chicago: University Chicago Press.

Althaus-Reid, Marcella, and Lisa Isherwood. 2007. "Thinking Theology and Queer Theory." *Feminist Theology* 15(3), 302–14.

An-Na'im, Abdullahi A. 2006. "Why Should Muslims Abandon Jihad? Human Rights and the Future of International Law." *Third World Quarterly* 27(5), 785–97.

——, ed. 1992. *Human Rights in Cross-Cultural Perspectives: A Quest for Consensus.* Philadelphia: University of Pennsylvania Press.

Aguiling-Pangalangan, Elizabeth. 2010. "Catholic Fundamentalism and Its Impact on Women's Political Participation in the Philippines." In *Religious Fundamentalisms and Their Gendered Impacts in Asia.* Ed. Claudia Derichs and Andrea Fleschenberg. Berlin: Friedrich-Ebert-Stiftung, 88–106.

Ameli, Saied Reza. 2012. *Bibliographical Discourse Analysis: The Western Academic Perspective on Islam, Muslims and Islamic Countries (1949–2009).* London: Islamic Human Rights Commission. Vols. 1–4.

Aquinas, Thomas. 1948. *Summa Theologica.* New York: Benzinger Brothers.

Aquino, María Pilar, ed. 1988. *Aportes para una teología desde la mujer/colaboraciones de teólogas latinoamericanas en la Conferencia Intercontinental de Mujeres Teólogas del Tercer Mundo.* Madrid: Biblia y Fe.

——. 1996. *Nosso clamor pela vida: Teologia latino-americana a partir da perspectiva da mulher.* São Paulo: Paulinas.

Aquino, María Pilar, and Maria José Rosado-Nunes. 2007. *Feminist Intercultural Theology: Latina Explorations for a Just World.* Maryknoll, NY: Orbis.

Archer, R. 2001. "Secularism and Sectarianism in India and the West: What Are the Real Lessons of American History?" *Economy and Society* 30(3), 273–87.

Arendt, Hannah. 1951. *The Origins of Totalitarianism.* New York: Harcourt, Brace & Co.

——. 1990. *On Revolution.* London: Penguin.

Arjomand, Said Amir, ed. 1984. *From Nationalism to Revolutionary Islam.* Albany: State University of New York Press.

——. 1993. *The Political Dimensions of Religion.* Albany: State University of New York Press.

Arokiasamy, G., and G. Gispert-Sauch, eds. 1987. *Liberation in Asia: Theological Perspectives.* Anand, Gujarat: Gujarat Sahitya Prakash; Delhi: Vidyajyoti, Faculty of Theology.

Arthur, Maria José, Teresa Cruz e Silva, Yolanda Sitoe, and Edson Mussa. 2011. "Lei da Família (1): Antecedentes e contextos da sua aprovação." *Outras Vozes* 35/36, 15–25.

Asad, Talal. 1993. *Genealogies of Religion: Discipline and Reasons of Power in Christianity and Islam.* Baltimore, MD: Johns Hopkins University Press.

——. 2003. *Formations of the Secular: Christianity, Islam, Modernity.* Stanford, CA: Stanford University Press.

Assmann, Hugo, and Franz Josef Hinkelammert. 1989. *A idolatria do mercado: Ensaio sobre economia e teologia.* Petrópolis, Brazil: Vozes.

Ateek, Naim Stifan. 1989. *Justice, and Only Justice: A Palestinian Theology of Liberation.* Maryknoll, NY: Orbis.

Ateek, Naim, Cedar Duaybis, and Maurine Tobin, eds. 2005. *Challenging Christian Zionism: Theology, Politics and the Israel-Palestine Conflict.* London: Melisende.

Ayoub, Mahmoud. 1995. "Jesus the Son of God: A Study of the Terms *Ibn* and *Walad* in the Qu'ran and Tafsir Tradition." In *Christian-Muslim Encounters*. Ed. Yvonne Yazbeck Haddad and Wadi Zaidan Haddad. Gainesville: University Press of Florida, 65–81.

Badran, Margot. 2009. *Feminism in Islam: Secular and Religious Convergences*. Oxford: Oneworld.

Barlas, Asma. 2002. *"Believing Women" in Islam: Unreading Patriarchal Interpretations of the Qur'an*. Austin: University of Texas Press.

———. 2006. "Does the Qu'ran Support Gender Equality? Or, do I have the autonomy to answer this question?" Workshop in Islam and Autonomy. University of Groningen, November 24. Available at *http://www.asmabarlas.com/TALKS/Groningen_Keynote .pdf* (accessed October 27, 2014).

Barzilai-Nahon, Karine, and Gad Barzilai. 2005. "Cultured Technology: The Internet and Religious Fundamentalism." *Information Society* 21(1), 25–40.

Bayes, Jane H., and Nayereh Tohidi. 2001. *Globalization, Gender, and Religion: The Politics of Women's Rights in Catholic and Muslim Contexts*. New York: Palgrave.

Bell, Jr., Daniel. 2004. "State and Civil Society." In *The Blackwell Companion to Political Theology*. Ed. Peter Scott and William Cavanaugh. Oxford: Blackwell, 423–38.

Benjamin, Walter. 1977. *Illuminations*. Ed. and Intro. Hannah Arendt. New York: Schocken Books.

Bergesch, Karen. 2006. *A dinâmica do poder na relação de violência doméstica: Desafios para o aconselhamento pastoral*. São Leopoldo, Brazil: Sinodal.

Betz, Hans-Georg, and Susan Meret. 2009. "Revisiting Lepanto: The Political Mobilization against Islam in Contemporary Western Europe." *Patterns of Prejudice* 43(3–4), 313–34.

Bhargava, Rajeev, ed. 1998. *Secularism and Its Critics*. New Delhi: Oxford University Press.

Bloch, Ernst. [1947] 1995. *The Principle of Hope*. Cambridge, MA: MIT Press.

Boff, Clodóvis. 1978. *Teologia e prática: Teologia do político e suas mediações*. Petrópolis, Brazil: Vozes.

———. 1984. *Teologia pé no chão*. Petrópolis, Brazil: Vozes.

———. 1998. *Teoria do método teológico*. Petrópolis, Brazil: Vozes.

Boff, Leonardo. 1973. *O destino do homem e do mundo; Ensaio sobre a vocação humana*. Petrópolis, Brazil: Vozes.

———. 1986. *Ecclesiogenesis: The Base Communities Reinvent the Church*. Maryknoll, NY: Orbis.

———. 1997. *Cry of the Earth, Cry of the Poor*. Maryknoll, NY: Orbis.

Bonate, Liazzat. 2006. "Matriliny, Islam and Gender." *Journal of Religion in Africa* 2(36), 139–66.

———. 2007a. "Roots of Diversity in Mozambican Islam." *Lusotopie* 19(1), 129–49.

———. 2007b. "Traditions and Transitions: Islam and Chiefship in Northern Mozambique. ca. 1850–1974." Dissertation submitted for the degree of Doctor of Philosophy. University of Cape Town.

Borges, Anselmo. 2010. *Religião e diálogo inter-religioso*. Coimbra: Imprensa da Universidade de Coimbra.

Brouwer, Steve Paul, and Susan Rose. 1996. *Exporting the American Gospel: Global Christian Fundamentalism.* New York: Routledge.

Brown, Candy Gunther, ed. 2011. *Global Pentecostal and Charismatic Healing.* New York: Oxford University Press.

Bruce, Steve. 1990. "Modernity and Fundamentalism: The New Christian Right in America." *British Journal of Sociology* 41, 477–96.

Budiman, Manneke. 2008. "Treading the Path of the Shari'a: Indonesian Feminism at the Crossroads of Western Modernity and Islamism." *Journal of Indonesian Social Sciences and Humanities* 1, 73–93.

Bultmann, Rudolf. 1984. *New Testament and Mythology and Other Basic Writings.* Ed. Schubert M. Ogden. Philadelphia: Fortress.

Burke, Roland. 2010. *Decolonization and the Evolution of International Human Rights.* Philadelphia: University of Pennsylvania Press.

Camus, Jean-Yves. 2007. "The European Extreme Right and Religious Extremism," *Central European Political Studies Review* 4, 263–79.

Casanova, J. 1994. *Public Religions in the Modern World.* Chicago: University of Chicago Press.

———. 2005. "Catholic and Muslim Politics in Comparative Perspective." *Taiwan Journal of Democracy* 1(2), 89–108.

———. 2011. "Cosmopolitanism, the Clash of Civilizations and Multiple Modernities." *Current Sociology* 59, 252–67.

Cheney, Kristen. 2012. "Locating Neocolonialism, 'Tradition,' and Human Rights in Uganda's 'Gay Death Penalty.'" *African Studies Review* 55(2), 77–95.

Christ, Carol. 1998. *Rebirth of the Goddess: Finding Meaning in Feminist Spirituality.* New York: Routledge.

———. 2004. *She Who Changes: Re-imagining the Divine in the World.* New York: Palgrave McMillan.

Co, Maria Anicia. 2013. "Some Perspectives on Fundamentalism and Its Impact on Youth." In *Youth in Asia: Challenges of Fundamentalism and Relativism.* Ed. Fr. Vimal Tirimanna. Federation of Asian Bishops' Conferences Papers (FABC), 135, 3–41. Available at http://www.fabc.org/fabc%20papers/fabc_papers%20135.pdf (accessed October 27, 2014).

Coene, Gily, and Chia Longman, eds. 2010. *Féminisme et multiculturalisme. Les paradoxes du débat.* Brussels: Peter Lang.

Coleman, Simon. 2000. *The Globalization of Charismatic Christianity: Spreading the Gospel of Prosperity.* Cambridge: Cambridge University Press.

Comaroff, Jean. 2009. "The Politics of Conviction. Faith on the Neo-liberal Frontier." *Social Analysis* 53(1), 17–38.

Cone, James. 1969. *Black Theology and Black Power.* New York: Seabury.

———. 1972. *The Spirituals and the Blues.* New York: Seabury.

Connolly, William. 1999. *Why I Am Not a Secularist.* Minneapolis: University of Minnesota Press.

Corten, Andre, and Ruth Marshall-Fratani, eds. 2001. *Between Babel and Pentecost:*

Transnational Pentecostalism in Africa and Latin America. Bloomington and Indianapolis: Indiana University Press.

Crossan, John. 1991. *The Historical Jesus: The Life of a Mediterranean Jewish Peasant.* New York: HarperCollins.

Dabashi, Hamid. 1993. *Theology of Discontent: The Ideological Foundations of the Islamic Revolution in Iran.* New York: New York University Press.

———. 2008. *Islamic Liberation Theology: Resisting the Empire.* New York: Routledge.

Daly, Mary. 1968. *The Church and the Second Sex.* Boston: Beacon.

———. 1973. *Beyond God the Father: Toward a Philosophy of Women's Liberation.* Boston: Beacon.

Daulatzai, Anila. 2004. "A Leap of Faith: Thoughts on Secularistic Practices and Progressive Politics." *International Social Science Journal* 56(182), 565–76.

David, Suh Kwang-Sun. 1983. "A Bibliographical Sketch of an Asian Theological Consultation." *Minjung Theology: People as the Subjects of History.* Commission on Theological Concerns of the Christian Conference of Asia. Maryknoll, NY: Orbis.

Davidson, Carl, and Jerry Harris. 2006. "Globalisation, Theocracy and the New Fascism: The US Right's Rise to Power." *Race & Class* 47(3), 47–67.

Donohue, J., and John L. Esposito, eds. 1982. *Islam in Transition: Muslim Perspectives.* New York: Oxford University Press.

Dube, Musa W., Andrew Mbuvi, and Dora Mbuwayesango, eds. 2012. *Postcolonial Perspectives in African Biblical Interpretations.* Atlanta, GA: Society of Biblical Literature.

Duchrow, Ulrich. 2006. "Dificultades y oportunidades para la teología en el mundo actual." In *Teología para otro mundo posible.* Ed. J. J. Tamayo and L. C. Susin. Madrid: PPC, 201–8.

Duderija, Adis. 2010. "The Interpretational Implications of Progressive Muslims' Qur'an and Sunna Manhaj in Relation to Their Formulation of a Normative Muslim Construct." *Islam and Christian-Muslim Relations* 19(4), 411–29.

Dupuis, Jacques. 1997. *Toward a Christian Theology of Religious Pluralism.* Maryknoll, NY: Orbis.

Dussel, Enrique. 1999. *Teologia da libertação—Um panorama do seu desenvolvimento.* Petrópolis, Brazil: Vozes.

———. 2006. *De Medellin a Puebla: Uma década de sangue.* São Paulo: Loyola.

Ebadi, Shirin. 2006. *Iran Awakening: A Memoir of Revolution and Hope.* New York: Random House.

Eberhard, Christoph. 2002. *Droit de l'homme et dialogue interculturel.* Paris: Écrivains.

Edwin, Shirin. 2006. "We Belong Here, Too: Accommodating African Muslim Feminism in African Feminist Theory via Zaynab Alkali's The Virtuous Woman and The Cobwebs and Other Stories." *Frontiers: A Journal of Women Studies* 27(3), 140–56.

Eickelman, Dale, and James Piscatori. 2004. *Muslim Politics.* Princeton: Princeton University Press.

Elizondo, Virgilio. 1975. *Christianity and Culture: An Introduction to Pastoral Theology and Ministry for the Bicultural Community.* Huntington, IN: Our Sunday Visitor.

————. 1977. "Teorías económicas y relación entre cristianismo y Socialismo." *Concilium* 125, 282–90.

————. 1990. *Mysterium liberationis. Conceptos fundamentales de teología de la liberación.* With Jon Sobrino. Madrid: Trotta.

Ellis, Mark H. 2004. *Toward a Jewish Theology of Liberation.* Waco, TX: Baylor University Press.

Ellis, Stephen, and Gerrie Ter Haar. 2007. "Religion and Politics: Taking African Epistemologies Seriously." *Journal of Modern African Studies* 45(3), 385–402.

Emerson, Michael O., and David Hartman. 2006. "The Rise of Religious Fundamentalism." *Annual Review of Sociology* 32, 127–44.

Engineer, Asghar Ali. 1990. *Islam and Liberation Theology: Essays on Liberative Elements in Islam.* New Delhi: Sterling.

————. 1998. *Rethinking Issues in Islam.* Mumbai: Orient Longman.

Ernst, Carl. 2006. *Sufism, Islam, and Globalization in the Contemporary World: Methodological Reflections on a Changing Field of Study.* Fourth Victor Danner Memorial Lecture, Indiana University, 15 April 2006.

Erskine, Noel. 1998. *Decolonizing Theology: A Caribbean Perspective.* Trenton, NJ: Africa World.

Essien, Anthonia M. 2004. *The Goodnews Community International: The Social Significance of Pentecostalism in a Changing Society.* Lagos: African Heritage Publications.

Evans, James. 1987. *Black Theology: A Critical Assessment and Annotated Bibliography.* New York: Greenwood.

Ezzat, Heba Raouf. 2001. "The Silent Ayesha: An Egyptian Narrative." In *Globalization, Gender, and Religion: The Politics of Women's Rights in Catholic and Muslim Contexts.* Ed. J. H. Bayes and Nayereh Tohidi. New York: Palgrave, 231–57.

Fabella, Virginia, and Mercy Amba Oduyoye. 1998. *With Passion and Compassion: Third World Women Doing Theology.* Eugene, OR: Wipf and Stock.

Falwell, Jerry. 1980. *Listen America!* New York: Doubleday.

Fasheh, Munir. 1992. "Reclaiming Our Identity and Redefining Ourselves." In *Faith and the Intifada: Palestinian Christian Voices.* Ed. Naim Ateek, Marc Ellis, and Rosemary Radford Ruether. Maryknoll, NY: Orbis, 61–70.

Feuerbach, Ludwig. [1841] 1957. *The Essence of Christianity.* New York: Harper.

Fiorenza, Elisabeth Schüssler. 1984. *In Memory of Her: A Feminist Theological Reconstruction of Christian Origins.* New York: Crossroads.

————. 1992. *But She Said: Feminist Practices of Biblical Interpretation.* Boston: Beacon.

————. 1993. *Discipleship of Equals: A Critical Feminist Ecclesia-logy of Liberation.* New York: Crossroads.

————. 1994. "Gewalt gegen Frauen." *Concilium. Internationale Zeitschrift für Theologie* 30(2), 95–107.

————. 1998. *Sharing Her Word: Feminist Biblical Interpretation in Context.* Boston: Beacon.

————. 2011. *Transforming Vision: Explorations in Feminist Theology.* Minneapolis: Augsburg Fortress.

Fischer, Michael. 1980. *Iran: From Religious Dispute to Revolution.* Cambridge, MA: Harvard University Press.

Fitzpatrick, Peter. 2007. "'What Are the Gods to Us Now?': Secular Theology and the Modernity of Law." *Theoretical Inquiries in Law* 8, 161–90.

Fletcher, Madeleine. 2006. "How Can We Understand Islamic Law Today?" *Islam and Christian-Muslim Relations* 17(2), 159–72.

Fornet-Betancourt, Raúl. 2006. *La interculturalidad a prueba.* Mainz, Germany: Verlag Mainz.

Foucault, Michel. 1976. *La volonté de savoir.* Paris: Gallimard.

———. 1977. *Discipline and Punish: The Birth of the Prison.* New York: Pantheon.

———. 1980. *Power and Knowledge.* New York: Pantheon.

Gaines, Edwene. 2005. *The Four Spiritual Laws of Prosperity: A Simple Guide to Unlimited Abundance.* New York: Rodale.

Garwood, Shae. 2005. "Politics at Work: Transnational Advocacy Networks and the Global Garment Industry." *Gender and Development* 13(3), 21–33.

Gebara, Ivone. 1998. *Teologia ecofeminista: Ensaio para repensar o conhecimento e a religião.* São Paulo: Olho d'Água.

Gifford, Paul. 2001. "The Complex Provenance of Some Elements of African Pentecostal Theology." In *Between Babel and Pentecost: Transnational Pentecostalism in Africa and Latin America.* Ed. André Corten and Ruth Marshall-Fratani. Bloomington: Indiana University Press, 62–79.

Gonzalez, Michelle A. 2004. "Who Is Americana/o?" In *Postcolonial Theologies: Divinity and Empire.* Ed. Catherine Keller, Michael Nausner, and Mayra Rivera. St. Louis: Chalice, 58–78.

———. 2006. *Afro-Cuban Theology: Religion, Race, Culture, and Identity.* Gainesville: University Press of Florida.

Goodale, Mark, ed. 2009a. *Human Rights: An Anthropological Reader.* Malden, MA: Wiley-Blackwell.

———. 2009b. *Surrendering to Utopia: An Anthropology of Human Rights.* Stanford, CA: Stanford University Press.

———. 2013. *Human Rights at the Crossroads.* New York: Oxford University Press.

Goodhart, Michael. 2013. "Human Rights and the Politics of Contestation." In *Human Rights at the Crossroads.* Ed. Mark Goodale. New York: Oxford University Press, 31–44.

Gordon, Lewis. 1995a. *Bad Faith and Antiblack Racism.* Atlantic Highlands, NJ: Humanities.

———. 1995b. *Fanon and the Crisis of European Man: An Essay on Philosophy and the Human Sciences.* New York: Routledge.

———. 2007. *Disciplinary Decadence: Living Thought in Trying Times.* Boulder, CO: Paradigm.

Gottwald, Norman K. 1979. *The Tribes of Yahweh: A Sociology of the Religion of Liberated Israel.* Maryknoll, NY: Orbis.

Green, John C. 2009. "American Faith-Based Politics in the Era of George W. Bush." *European Political Science* 8, 316–29.

Green, Nile. 2004. "Emerging Approaches to the Sufi Traditions of South Asia: Between Texts, Territories and the Transcendent." *South Asia Research* 24, 123–48.

Gresh, Alain. 2004. *L'Islam, la République et le monde*. Paris: Fayard.

Guerrero, Andrés Gonzales. 1987. *A Chicano Theology*. Maryknoll, NY: Orbis.

Gumbrecht, Hans Ulrich. 2004. *Production of Presence: What Meaning Cannot Convey*. Stanford, CA: Stanford University Press.

Gutiérrez, Gustavo. 1971. *Teología de la liberación. Perspectivas*. Lima: CEP.

———. 2004. *Acordarse de los pobres; Textos esenciales*. Lima: Fondo Editorial del Congreso del Peru.

Haddad, Yvonne Yazbeck, and Wadi Zaidan Haddad, eds. 1995. *Christian-Muslim Encounters*. Gainesville: University Press of Florida.

Hagin, Kenneth. 1985. *The Coming Restoration*. N.p.: RHEMA Bible Church.

Hallaq, Wael B. 2004. *Authority, Continuity and Change in Islamic Law*. Cambridge: Cambridge University Press.

Hetata, Sherif. 1989. "East-West Relations." *Islamic Fundamentalism: A Debate on the Role of Islam Today*. Ed. Nawal Saadawi et al. London: Institute for African Alternatives, 21–27.

Hick, John, and Paul Knitter, eds. 1987. *The Myth of Christian Uniqueness: Toward a Pluralistic Theology of Religions*. Maryknoll, NY: Orbis.

Hopwood, Derek, ed. 1999. *Arab Nation, Arab Nationalism*. New York: St. Martin's; Oxford: St. Antony's College.

Hurewitz, J. C., ed. 1975. *The Middle East and North Africa in World Politics*. New Haven, CT: Yale University Press.

Irudayaraj, Xavier, ed. 1990. *Emerging Dalit Theology*. Madras, India: Jesuit Theological Secretariate.

Isasi-Díaz, Ada María, and Yolanda Tarango. 1988. *Hispanic Women. Mujer Hispana. Prophetic Voice in the Church. Voz Profética en la Iglesia*. Scranton, PA: University of Scranton Press.

Joas, Hans. 2013. *The Sacredness of the Person: A New Genealogy of Human Rights*. Washington, DC: Georgetown University Press.

———. 2014. *Faith as an Option: Possible Futures for Christianity*. Stanford, CA: Stanford University Press.

John Paul II, Pope. 1991. *Encyclical Letter "Centesimus Annus."* Vatican: Vatican Ed.

Kamitsuka, Margaret. 2004. "Toward a Feminist Postmodern and Postcolonial Interpretation of Sin." *Journal of Religion* 84(2), 179–211.

Kang, Namsoon. 2004. "Who/What Is an Asian? A Postcolonial Theological Reading of Orientalism and Neo-Orientalism." In *Postcolonial Theologies. Divinity and Empire*. Ed. Catherine Keller, Michael Nausner, and Mayra Rivera. St. Louis, MO: Chalice, 100–117.

Karam, Azza. 1998. *Women, Islamisms and the State: Contemporary Feminisms in Egypt*. London and New York: Macmillan and St. Martin's Press.

Keck, Margaret, and Kathryn Sikkink. 1998. *Activists Beyond Borders: Advocacy Networks in International Politics.* Ithaca, NY: Cornell University Press.

Keller, Catherine, Michael Nausner, and Mayra Rivera, eds. 2004. *Postcolonial Theologies: Divinity and Empire.* St. Louis, MO: Chalice.

Khalidi, Tarif, ed. 2001. *The Muslim Jesus: Sayings and Stories in Islamic Literature.* Cambridge, MA: Harvard University Press.

King, Ursula, ed. 1994. *Feminist Theology from the Third World.* Maryknoll, NY: Orbis.

Knitter, Paul. 2002. *Introducing Theologies of Religions.* Maryknoll, NY: Orbis.

Kumari, Prasanna, ed. 1999. *Feminist Theology: Perspectives and Praxis: Gurukul Summer Institute, 1998.* Chennai, India: Gurukul Lutheran Theological College & Research Institute.

Küng, Hans. 2010. "Peace Proposal." Available at http://www.peaceproposal.com/Kung .html (accessed October 27, 2014).

Kunnie, Julian. 1994. *Models of Black Theology: Issues in Class, Culture, and Gender.* Valley Forge, PA: Trinity Press International.

Kuttab, Jonathan. 1992. "Biblical Justice, Law, and the Occupation." *Faith and the Intifada: Palestinian Christian Voices.* Ed. Naim Ateek, Marc Ellis, and Rosemary Radford Ruether. Maryknoll, NY: Orbis, 93–96.

Laski, Harold. 1948. "Toward a Declaration of Human Rights." In *UNESCO Human Rights: Comments and Interpretations* (with an introduction by Jacques Maritain), Paris, 65–79. Available at http://unesdoc.unesco.org/images/0015/001550/155042eb .pdf (accessed October 27, 2014).

Lathuilière, Pierre. 1995. *Le fondamentalisme catholique.* Paris: Les Éditions du Cerf.

Le Gall, Dina. 2010. "Recent Thinking on Sufis and Saints in the Lives of Muslim Societies, Past and Present." *International Journal of Middle East Studies* 42, 673–87.

Lehmann, David. 1998. "Fundamentalism and Globalism." *Third World Quarterly* 19, 607–34.

Leite, António Pinto. 2012. *O amor como critério de gestão.* Lisbon: Principia.

Libânio, J. B. 1999. "Panorama da teologia da América Latina nos últimos anos." *Revista Electrónica Latinoamericana de Teología (RELaT).* Available at http://www.servicio skoinonia.org/relat/ (accessed October 27, 2014).

Loades, Ann, ed. 1990. *Feminist Theology: A Reader.* London: Society for Promoting Christian Knowledge.

Löwy, Michael. 1996. *The War of Gods: Religion and Politics in Latin America.* London; New York: Verso.

Macdonald, Duncan. 1903. *Development of Muslim Theology, Jurisprudence, and Constitutional Theory.* New York: Charles Scribner's.

Macpherson, C. B. 1962. *The Political Theory of Possessive Individualism: Hobbes to Locke.* Oxford: Clarendon Press.

Madigan, Patricia. 2010. "Women Negotiating Modernity: A Gender Perspective on Fundamentalisms in Catholicism and Islam." *Islam and Christian-Muslim Relations* 20(1), 1–20.

Maier, Charles. 1993. "A Surfeit of Memory? Reflections on History, Melancholy and Denial." *History and Memory* 5(2), 136–52.

Maldonado-Torres, Nelson. 2006. "The Time of History, the Time of Gods, and the Damnés de la Terre." *Worlds & Knowledges Otherwise* 1(2), 1–12.

Mannot, C., and X. Ternisien. 2003. "Tariq Ramadan Accused of Anti-Semitism." *Watch*, October 14.

Marcos, Sylvia. 2002. "Körper und Geschlecht in mesoamerikanischen Religionen." *Concilium. Internationale Zeitschrift für Theologie* 38(2), 201–12.

Marramao, Giacomo. 1994. *Cielo e terra. Genealogia della secolarizzazione*. Rome: Bari.

Marsden, George M. 2006. *Fundamentalism and American Culture*. Oxford: Oxford University Press.

Marx, Karl. [1843] 1964. *Early Writings (A Contribution to the Critique of Hegel's Philosophy of Right)*. Trans. T. Bottomore. New York: McGraw-Hill.

———. [1843] 1977. "On the Jewish Question." In *Karl Marx: Selected Writings*. Ed. David McLellan. Oxford: Oxford University Press, 39–62.

McFague, Sally. 2000. *Life Abundant: Rethinking Theology and Economy for a Planet in Peril*. Minneapolis: Augsburg Fortress.

———. 2008. *A New Climate for Theology: God, the World, and Global Warming*. Minneapolis: Augsburg Fortress.

Merali, Arzu, and Javad Sharbaf, eds. 2009. *Towards a New Liberation Theology: Reflections on Palestine*. Papers presented at conference of same title, June 2005. London: Islamic Human Rights Commission.

Mernissi, Fatima. 1987. *Beyond the Veil: Male-Female Dynamics in Modern Muslim Society*. Bloomington: Indiana University Press.

———. 1991. *The Veil and the Male Elite: A Feminist Interpretation of Women's Rights in Islam*. New York: Perseus.

———. 1996. *Women's Rebellion and Islamic Memory*. London: Zed.

Merry, Sally Engle. 2006. *Human Rights and Gender Violence: Translating International Law into Local Justice*. Chicago: University of Chicago Press.

Metz, Johann. 1968. "The Church's Social Function in the Light of a 'Political Theology.'" In *Faith and the World of Politics*. Ed. Johann Metz. New York: Paulist, 2–18.

———. 1980. *Faith in History and Society: Toward a Practical Fundamental Theology*. New York: Seabury.

Meyer, Birgit. 2004. "Christianity in Africa: From African Independent to Pentecostal-Charismatic Churches." *Annual Review of Anthropology* 33, 447–74.

Mir-Hosseini, Ziba. 1996. "Stretching the Limits: A Feminist Reading of the Shari'a in Post-Khomeini Iran." In *Feminism and Islam: Legal and Literary Perspectives*. Ed. Mai Yamani. New York: New York University Press, 285–319.

———. 2006. "Muslim Women's Quest for Equality: Between Islamic Law and Feminism." *Critical Inquiry* 32(4), 629–45.

Modood, Tariq. 2003. "Muslims and the Politics of Difference." *Political Quarterly* 74(s1), 100–115.

Moghadam, V. M. 2002. "Islamic Feminism and Its Discontents: Toward a Resolution of the Debate." *Signs: Journal of Women in Culture and Society* 27(4), 1135–71.

Mohanty, Chandra Tapade. 1991. "Under Western Eyes: Feminist Scholarship and Colonial Discourses." In *Third World Women and the Politics of Feminism*. Ed. Chandra Tapade Mohanty, Ann Russo, and Lourdes Torres. Bloomington: Indiana University Press, 255–77.

Mojab, Shahrzad. 2001. "Theorizing the Politics of 'Islamic Feminism.'" *Feminist Review* 69, 124–46.

Moltmann, Jurgen. 1967. *Theology of Hope: On the Ground and the Implications of a Christian Eschatology.* London: Supply Chain Management.

———. 1982. *The Power of the Powerless.* San Francisco: Harper & Row.

Moosa, Ebrahim. 2000. "Introduction." In *Revival and Reform in Islam: A Study of Islamic Fundamentalism.* Ed. Fazlur Rahman. Oxford: Oneworld, 1–29.

———. 2004. "The Dilemma of Islamic Rights Schemes." *Worlds and Knowledges Otherwise,* 1(1), 1–25. Available at http://www.jhfc.duke.edu/wko/dossiers/1.1/MoosaE.pdf (accessed October 27, 2014).

———. 2005. *Ghazali and the Poetics of Imagination.* Chapel Hill, London: University of North Carolina Press.

———. 2006. "'Transitions in the 'Progress' of Civilization: Theorizing History, Practice and Tradition." *Voices of Islam.* Ed. V. J. Cornell, V. G. Henry-Blakemore, and O. Safi. Westport: Praeger, 115–30.

———. 2008. "Social Change." In *The Islamic World.* Ed. Andrew Rippin. London: Routledge, 565–75.

Moyn, Samuel. 2010. *The Last Utopia: Human Rights in History.* Cambridge, MA: Harvard University Press.

Murray, Kyle. 2012. "Christian 'Renewalism' and the Production of Global Free Market Hegemony." *International Politics* 49(2), 260–76.

Nagata, Judith. 2001. "Beyond Theology: Toward an Anthropology of 'Fundamentalism.'" *American Anthropologist New Series* 103(2), 481–98.

Nandy, Ashis. 1985. "An Anti-Secularist Manifesto." *Seminar* 314, 1–12.

———. 1998. "The Politics of Secularism and the Recovery of Religious Tolerance." *Secularism and Its Critics.* Ed. Rajev Bhargava. New Delhi: Oxford University Press, 321–44.

New, David. 2012. *Christian Fundamentalism in America: A Cultural History.* Jefferson, MO: McFarland & Co.

Nietzsche, Friedrich. [1882] 1974. *The Gay Science: With a Prelude in Rhymes and an Appendix of Songs.* Trans. Walter Kaufmann. New York: Vintage.

———. [1883] 2012. "The Despisers of the Body." In *Thus Also Spoke Zarathustra.* Trans. Thomas Common. A Project Gutenberg e-Book. Available at http://www.gutenberg.org/files/1998/1998-h/1998-h.htm#link2H_4_0004 (accessed October 27, 2014).

North, Gary. n.d. *What Is The ICE?* Available at http://www.garynorth.com/freebooks/whatsice.htm *(accessed* October 27, 2014).

———. 1997. "The Wealth of Nations." *Biblical Economics Today,* 18(2). Available at http://www.reformed-theology.org/ice/newslet/bet/bet97.02.htm *(accessed* October 27, 2014).

Novak, Michael. 1982. *The Spirit of Democratic Capitalism.* New York: Simon & Schuster.

Obadare, Ebenezer. 2006. "Pentecostal Presidency? The Lagos-Ibadan 'Theocratic' Class and the Muslim 'Other.'" *Review of African Political Economy* 110, 665–78.

Okin, Susan Moller. 1999. *Is Multiculturalism Bad for Women?* Princeton, NJ: Princeton University Press.

Özsoy, Ömer. 2006. "Darf der Koran historisch-hermeneutisch gelesen werden?" In *Der Islam in Europa. Zwischen Weltpolitik und Alltag.* Ed. Urs Altermatt, Mariano Delgado, and Guido Vergauwen. Stuttgart: W. Kohlhammer, 153–75.

Panikkar, Raimundo. 1988. "The Jordan, the Tiber, and the Ganges: Three Kairological Moments of Christic Self-Consciousness." In *The Myth of Christian Uniqueness.* Ed. John Hick and Paul F. Knitter. London: Supply Chain Management, 89–116.

———. 2011. "Freeing Christian Faith from the Bonds of Western Culture." *The Attentive Voice: Reflections on the Meaning and Practice of Interreligious Dialogue.* Ed. William Skudlarek. Brooklyn, NY: Lantern.

Pascal, Blaise. 1966. *Pensées.* Trans. A. J. Krailsheimer. London: Penguin.

Pereira, Nancy Cardoso. 2002. "Der Bewegungslose Tanz. Körper und Bible in Lateinamerika." *Concilium. Internationale Zeitschrift für Theologie* 38(2), 178–86.

Perry, Michael. 1997. *Religion in Politics: Constitutional and Moral Perspectives.* New York: Oxford University Press.

Pew Forum on Religion and Public Life. 2012. "How the Faithful Voted: 2012 Preliminary Analysis." ANALYSIS November 7. Available at http://www.pewforum.org/2012/11/07/how-the-faithful-voted-2012-preliminary-exit-poll-analysis/ (accessed October 27, 2014).

Polanyi, Karl. 1944. *The Great Transformation.* Boston: Beacon Press.

Polanyi, Michael. 1962. *Personal Knowledge.* Chicago: University of Chicago Press.

Pratt, Douglas. 2010. "Religion and Terrorism: Christian Fundamentalism and Extremism." *Terrorism and Political Violence* 22(3), 438–56.

Pratt, Mary Louise. 1992. *Imperial Eyes: Travel Writing and Transculturation.* London: Routledge.

Pui-lan, Kwok. 2005. *Postcolonial Imagination and Feminist Theology.* Louisville, KY: Westminster John Knox.

Queiruga, Andrés. 1987. *La revelación de dios en la realización del hombre.* Madrid: Cristiandad.

Raheb, Mitri. 1995. *I am a Palestinian Christian.* Trans. R.C.L. Gritsch. Minneapolis: Augsburg Fortress.

Rahman, Fazlur. 1982. *Islam and Modernity: Transformation of an Intellectual Tradition.* Chicago: University Chicago Press.

———. 2000. *Revival and Reform in Islam: A Study of Islamic Fundamentalism.* Oxford: Oneworld.

Ramadan, Tariq. 2002. *To Be a European Muslim: A Study of Islamic Sources in the European Context.* Leicester, UK: Islamic Foundation.

———. 2004. *Western Muslims and the Future of Islam*. New York: Oxford University Press.

———. 2005a. "El papel de las religiones ante los problemas sociales y políticos: Respuesta al professor Hans Küng." In *Interculturalidad, diálogo interreligioso y liberación*. Ed. Juan José Tamayo and Raul Fornet-Betancourt. Navarre, Spain: Verbo Divino, 31–40.

———. 2005b. *"Les Musulmans et la laïcité" 1905–2005: Les enjeux de la laïcité*. Paris: L'Harmattan.

Ratzinger, Joseph. 1993. *A igreja e a nova europa*. Lisbon: Verbo.

Razack, Sherene H. 2004. "Imperilled Muslim Women, Dangerous Muslim Men and Civilised Europeans: Legal and Social Responses to Forced Marriages." *Feminist Legal Studies,* 12, 129–74.

———. 2007. "The 'Sharia Law Debate' in Ontario: The Modernity/Premodernity Distinction in Legal Efforts to Protect Women from Culture." *Feminist Legal Studies* 15, 3–32.

Ress, Mary Judith. 2006. *Ecofeminism in Latin America*. Maryknoll, NY: Orbis.

Rivera, Mayra. 2007. *The Touch of Transcendence: A Postcolonial Theology of God*. Louisville, KY: Westminster John Knox Press.

Robson, Laura C. 2010. "Palestinian Liberation Theology, Muslim-Christian Relations and the Arab-Israeli Conflict." *Islam and Christian-Muslim Relations* 21(1), 39–50.

Rosenberger, Sieglinde, and Leila Hadj-Abdou. 2013. "Islam at Issue: Anti-Islamic Mobilization of the Extreme Right in Austria." In *Varieties of Right-Wing Extremism in Europe*. Ed. Andrea Mammone, Emmanuel Godin, and Brian Jenkins. New York: Routledge, 149–63.

Rouhana, Hoda. 2005. "Women Living under Muslim Laws (WLUML) Network's Understanding of Religious Fundamentalisms and Its Responses." *Muslim Women and the Challenge of Islamic Extremism*. Ed. Norani Othman. Kuala Lumpur, Malaysia: Sisters in Islam, 178–95.

Roy, Olivier. 1994. *The Failure of Political Islam*. Cambridge, MA: Harvard University Press.

Ruether, Rosemary Radford. 1991. "Redemptive Community in Christianity." *Buddhist-Christian Studies* 11, 217–30.

———. 1993. *Sexism and God Talk: Toward a Feminist Theology*. Boston: Beacon.

———. 2011. *Women and Redemption: A Theological History*. Minneapolis: Augsburg Fortress.

Ruthven, Malise. 2007. *Fundamentalism: A Very Short Introduction*. Oxford: Oxford University Press.

Saadawi, Nawal, and Sherif Hetata. 1999. "Political Islam and Democracy." Paper presented at the Conference on Religion and Democracy, Mansfield College, Oxford, September 10–12. Available at *http:/* www.nawalsaadawi.net/articlessherif/articles/polislam.htm (accessed October 27, 2014).

Sadowsky, Yahya. 2006. "Political Islam: Asking the Wrong Questions?" *Annual Review of Political Science* 9, 215–240.

Safi, Omid. 2005. "A Scent from the Garden of Ancients: A Modern Muslim's Musing on the Classics of Western Spirituality Series." *Spiritus* 5, 107–10.

Sahgal, Gita, and Nira Yuval-Davis. 1992. "Introduction: Fundamentalism, Multiculturalism and Women in Britain." In *Refusing Holy Orders: Women and Fundamentalism in Britain*. Ed. Gita Sahgal and Nira Yuval-Davis. London: Virago, 1–25.

Said, Edward. 1978. *Orientalism*. New York: Pantheon Books.

Salime, Zadike. 2011. *Between Feminism and Islam*. Minneapolis: University of Minnesota Press.

Santos, Boaventura de Sousa. 1995. *Toward a New Common Sense: Law, Science and Politics in the Paradigmatic Transition*. London: Routledge.

———. 1998. "The Fall of the Angelus Novus: Beyond the Modern Game of Roots and Options." *Current Sociology* 46(2), 81–118.

———. 2002a. "The Processes of Globalization." *Eurozine* 68(14).

———. 2002b. *Toward a New Legal Common Sense: Law, Globalization, and Emancipation*. London: Butterworths.

———. 2004. "A Critique of Lazy Reason: Against the Waste of Experience." In *The Modern World-System in the Longue Durée*. Ed. I. Wallerstein. Boulder, CO: Paradigm, 157–97.

———. 2006a. *A gramática do tempo*. Oporto: Afrontamento.

———. 2006b. *The Rise of the Global Left: The World Social Forum and Beyond*. London: Zed.

———. 2007a. "Beyond Abyssal Thinking: From Global Lines to Ecologies of Knowledges." *Review Fernand Braudel Center* 30(1), 45–89.

———, ed. 2007b. *Cognitive Justice in a Global World: Prudent Knowledge for a Decent Life*. Lanham, MD: Lexington.

———. 2007c. "Human Rights as an Emancipatory Script? Cultural and Political Conditions." In *Another Knowledge Is Possible*. Ed. B. S. Santos. London: Verso, 3–40.

———. 2008. "The World Social Forum and the Global Left." *Politics and Society* 36(2).

———. 2009. "If God Were a Human Rights Activist: Human Rights and the Challenge of Political Theologies." *Law, Social Justice & Global Development*, March 11.

———. 2010. *Refundación del estado en américa latina. Perspectivas desde una epistemología del sur*. La Paz: Plural.

———. 2014. *Epistemologies of the South: Justice against Epistemicide*. Boulder, CO: Paradigm.

Sayyid, Salman. 2003. *A Fundamental Fear: Eurocentrism and the Emergence of Islamism*. London; New York: Zed.

———. 2005. "Mirror, Mirror: Western Democrats, Oriental Despots?" *Ethnicities* 5(1), 30–50.

———. 2014. *Reclaiming the Caliphate: Decolonization and World Order*. London: Hurst.

Sayyid, Salman, and Abdoolkarim Vakil, eds. 2010. *Thinking through Islamophobia: Global Perspectives*. London: Hurst.

Schmitt, Carl. 1922. *Politische Theologie: Vier Kapitel zur Lehre von der Souveränität*. Berlin: n.p.

Schreiter, Robert J., ed. 1991. *Faces of Jesus in Africa*. Maryknoll, NY: Orbis.

Schuster, Ekkehard, and Reinhold Boschert-Kimmig. 1999. *Hope Against Hope: Johann Baptist Metz and Elie Wiesel Speak Out on the Holocaust*. New York: Paulist.

Scott, Peter, and William Cavanaugh, eds. 2004. *The Blackwell Companion to Political Theology*. Malden, MA: Blackwell.

Shahidian, Hammed. 2002. *Women in Iran: Gender Politics in the Islamic Republic*. Westport, CT: Greenwood.

Shah-Kazemi, Reza. 2006. *Paths to Transcendence: According to Shankara, Ibn Arabi, and Meister Eckhart*. Bloomington: World Wisdom.

Shaik, Sa'diyya. 2004. "Knowledge, Women and Gender in the Adīth: A Feminist Interpretation." *Knowledge, Women and Gender in the Adīth: A Feminist Interpretation, Islam and Christian-Muslim Relations* 15(1), 99–108.

Shariati, Ali. 1980. *Marxism and Other Western Fallacies: An Islamic Critique*. Berkeley, CA: Mizan.

———. 1986. *What Is to Be Done? The Enlightened Thinkers and an Islamic Renaissance*. North Haledon, NJ: Institute for Research and Islamic Studies.

———. 2002. *Where Shall We Begin? Enlightened Thinkers and the Revolutionary Society*. Penang: Citizens International.

Skenderovic, Damir. 2006. "Feindbild Muslime—Islamophobie in der radikalen Rechten." In *Der Islam in Europa. Zwischen Weltpolitik und Alltag*. Ed. Urs Altermatt, Mariano Delgado, and Guido Vergauwen. Stuttgart, Germany: W. Kohlhammer, 97–105.

Smith, Jackie. 2005. *Coalitions Across Borders*. Lanham, MD: Rowan & Littlefield.

Smith, Jackie, and Dawn Wiest. 2012. *Social Movements in the World-System*. New York: Russell Sage Foundation.

Sobrino, Jon. 1984. *Resurrección de la verdadera Iglesia. Los pobres, lugar teológico de la eclesiologia*. Santander, Spain: Sal Terrae.

———. 2007. *Fuera de los pobres no hay salvación: Pequeños ensayos utópico-proféticos*. Ellacuría Fundazioa.

Soelle, Dorothee. 1974. *Political Theology*. Philadelphia: Fortress.

———. 2006. *Essential Writings*. Maryknoll, NY: Orbis.

Solomon, Hussein, ed. 2005. *Islam in the 21st Century*. Pretoria: Centre for International Political Studies, University of Pretoria.

Spivak, Gayatri Chakravorty. 2002. "Resident Alien." In *Relocating Postcolonialism*. Ed. David Theo Goldberg and Ato Quayson. Oxford: Blackwell, 47–65.

Ströher, Marga Janéte. 2009. "Teologia feminista e gênero—territorialidades, deslocamentos e horizontes." *Presentations at the 3rd World Forum of Theology and Liberation*. Available at http://www.wftl.org/pdf/055.pdf (accessed October 27, 2014).

St. Ville, Susan M. 2012. "Befreinde Entsagung: Gedanken zur feministischen Spiritualität der Gegenwart." *Concilium. Internationale Zeitschrift für Theologie* 48(4), 445–52.

Sugirtharajah, R. S. 2002. *Postcolonial Criticism and Biblical Interpretation*. Oxford: Oxford University Press.

———. 2005. *The Bible and Empire: Postcolonial Exploitations*. Cambridge: Cambridge University Press.

Sung, Jung Mo. 2007. *Desire, Market and Religion (Reclaiming Liberation Theology)*. London: Supply Chain Management.

———. 2011a. "Religion und Ökonomie: Schnittstellen." *Concilium. Internationale Zeitschrifht für Theologie* 47(5), 482–91.

———. 2011b. *The Subject, Capitalism and Religion: Horizons of Hope in Complex Societies*. New York: Palgrave MacMillan.

Tamale, Sylvia. 2008. "The Right to Culture and the Culture of Rights: A Critical Perspective on Women's Sexual Rights in Africa." *Feminist Legal Studies* 16(1), 47–69.

———. 2009. "A Human Rights Impact Assessment of the Ugandan Anti-homosexuality Bill 2009." *Equal Rights Review* 4, 49–57.

Tamayo, Juan José. 1993. "Teologias de la liberation." *Conceptos fundamentales del cristianismo*. Ed. Juan José Tamayo. Madrid: Trotta, 1363–75.

———. 2003. "Würde und Befreiung: Eine theologisch-politische Betrachtung." *Concilium. Internationale Zeitschrift für Theologie* 39(2), 189–200.

———. 2004a. *Hacia la comunidad 5. Por eso lo mataron. El horizonte Ético de Jesús de Nazaret*. Madrid: Trotta.

———. 2004b. "Las teologías de Abya-Yala." *Teologías de Abya-Yala y formación teológica: Interacciones y desafíos*. 7ª Jornada Teológica. Bogotá: CETELA, 85–121.

———. 2005. "Introducción." In *Interculturalidad, diálogo interreligioso y liberación*. Ed. J. J. Tamayo and R. Fornet-Betancourt. I Simposio Internacional de Teología Intercultural e Interreligiosa de la Liberación. Barcelona, 11–12 de julio de 2004. Navarre, Spain: Verbo Divino, 9–13.

———. 2009. *Fundamentalismos y Diálogo entre Religiones*. Madrid: Trotta.

———. 2011. *Outra teología es possible: Pluralismo religioso, interculturalidad y feminismo*. Madrid: Herder.

Tamez, Elsa, and Michael O'Connell, eds. 2006. *Bible of the Oppressed*. Eugene, OR: Wipf and Stock.

Taylor, Charles. 2007. *A Secular Age*. Cambridge, MA: Belknap Press of Harvard University Press.

Taylor, Mark Lewis. 2004. "Spirit and Liberation: Achieving Postcolonial Theology in the United States." In *Postcolonial Theologies: Divinity and Empire*. Ed. Catherine Keller, Michael Nausner, and Mayra Rivera. St. Louis, MO: Chalice, 39–55.

Terretta, Meredith. 2012. "'We Had Been Fooled into Thinking that the UN Watches over the Entire World': Human Rights, UN Trust Territories, and Africa's Decolonization." *Human Rights Quarterly* 34(2), 329–60.

Thanzauva, K. 2002. *Transforming Theology: A Theological Basis for Social Transformation*. Bangalore, India: Asian Trading.

Theissen, Gerd, and Annette Merz. 1998. *The Historical Jesus: A Comprehensive Guide*. Minneapolis: Augsburg Fortress.

Theocracy Watch. 2005. "Dominionism and Dominion Theology." Available at http://www.theocracywatch.org/dominionism.htm (accessed October 27, 2014).

Tibi, Bassam. 2005. *Islam between Culture and Politics.* New York: Palgrave Macmillan.

Tohidi, N. 1997. "'Islamic Feminism': A Democratic Challenge or a Theocratic Reaction?" *Kankash: A Persian Journal of History, Culture, and Politics* 13.

Told, Michaela R. 2004. "Catholic Fundamentalism, Right-Wing Politics and the Construction of Womanhood: The Case of Austria." Available at http://www.wluml.org /sites/wluml.org/files/import/english/pubs/pdf/wsf/05.pdf (accessed October 27, 2014).

Toldy, Teresa. 2007. "Secularism in Europe: Conceptual Debates (introductory approach)." Paper presented at the conference Muslims in Europe and the Politics of Multiculturalism. Centro de Estudos Sociais, Coimbra, October 15.

———. 2011. "'Secularist Dreams' and 'Women's Rights': Notes on an 'Ambiguous Relationship.'" *RCCS Annual Review: An Online Journal for the Social Sciences and the Humanities* 3(October), 1–19.

———. 2012. "Sisterhood in Different Voices? Religion, Secularism and Women Rights." *Journal of the European Society of Women in Theological Research* 20, 59–86.

Ul-Haq, Mushir. 1982. "Islam in Secular India." In *Islam in Transition: Muslim Perspectives.* Ed. J. Donohue and John L. Esposito. New York: Oxford University Press, 175–77.

UNESCO, ed. 1948. *Human Rights: Comments and Interpretations; a symposium edited by UNESCO* (with an introduction by Jacques Maritain). Paris: UNESCO. Available at http://unesdoc.unesco.org/images/0015/001550/155042eb.pdf (accessed October 27, 2014).

Valentin, Benjamin. 2002. *Mapping Public Theology: Beyond Culture, Identity, and Difference.* Harrisburg, PA: Trinity Press International.

van Ess, Josef. 1991–1997. *Theologie und Gesellschaft im 2.und 3.Jahrhundert Hidschra.* (6 vols.) Berlin, New York: Walter de Gruyter.

———. 2006. *The Flowering of Muslim Theology.* Cambridge, MA: Harvard University Press.

Vuola, Elina. 2002. *Limits of Liberation: Feminist Theology and the Ethics of Poverty and Reproduction.* London; New York: Sheffield Academic.

Wadud, Amina. 1999. *Qur'an and Woman: Rereading the Sacred Text from a Woman's Perspective.* Oxford: Oxford University Press.

———. 2006. *Inside the Gender Jihad.* Oxford: Oneworld.

Weisberg, D. Kelly, ed. 1993. *Feminist Legal Theory: Foundations.* Philadelphia: Temple University Press.

Welch, Sharon D. 2000. *A Feminist Ethic of Risk.* Minneapolis: Augsburg Fortress.

Westerlund, David, and Ingvar Svanberg, eds. 1999. *Islam Outside the Arab World.* London: Routledge Curzon.

Wiesel, Elie. 1999. "The Perils of Indifference: Lessons Learned from a Violent Century." *Millennium Lecture Series.* White House, Washington DC. Available at http://www .pbs.org/eliewiesel/resources/millennium.html (accessed October 27, 2014).

Wilfred, Felix. 2000. *Asian Dreams and Christian Hope: At the Dawn of the Millennium.* New Delhi: Indian Society for Promoting Christian Knowledge.

———. 2002. *On the Banks of Ganges—Doing Contextual Theology*. New Delhi: Indian Society for Promoting Christian Knowledge.

———. 2009. *Dalit Empowerment*. New Delhi: Indian Society for Promoting Christian Knowledge.

Women's Theologians Fellowship. 2002. *Birthing a Burmese Feminist Theology: Feminist Theology Workshop, 8th–10th February, 2002, Jerusalem, Hmawbi*. Rangoon: Women's Theologians Fellowship, Association for Theological Education in Myanmar.

Yamani, Mai, ed. 1996. *Feminism and Islam: Legal and Literary Perspectives*. New York: New York University Press.

Young, L., and J. Everitt. 2004. *Advocacy Groups*. Vancouver: University of British Columbia Press.

Yuval-Davis, Nira. 1992. "Women's Empowerment and Jewish Fundamentalism." In *Refusing Holy Orders: Women and Fundamentalism in Britain*. Ed. Gita Sahgal and Nira Yuval-Davis. London: Virago, 198–226.

———. 1999. "The Personal Is Political: Jewish Fundamentalism and Women's Empowerment." *Religious Fundamentalisms and the Human Rights of Women*. Ed. Courtney W. Howland. Basingstoke, UK: Macmillan Press, 33–42.

———. 2004. "Jewish Fundamentalisms and Women." *Warning Signs of Fundamentalisms*. Ed. Ayesha Imam and Nira Yuval-Davis. London: Women Living under Muslim Laws, 27–32.

Index

CPSIA information can be obtained
at www.ICGtesting.com
Printed in the USA
JSHW022125130123
36289JS00001B/5